WALLET FULL

OF

MONEY

The Critical Factors that Determine

Unimaginable Wealth and Financial Success

Chad E. Tennant

Wallet Full of Money
Copyright © 2017 Chad E. Tennant
All rights reserved.

*****

Links to sources and references can be accessed directly from the e-book edition. The e-book is downloadable free of charge with the purchase of the paperback edition.

Categories: 1. Business 2. Money 3. Personal Finance 4. Education & Reference

CONTENTS

INTRODUCTION

More than one hundred years ago, in 1916, John D. Rockefeller arguably became the world's first confirmed US-dollar billionaire. Today, there are roughly two thousand billionaires, depending on which source you cite. *Forbes* started reporting on billionaires in 1987. Its initial report listed 140 billionaires, including ninety-six outside of the United States, and since then, Microsoft co-founder Bill Gates has frequently topped the list. A lot has changed in thirty years, with a growing interest and spotlight on the world's wealthiest. Individuals want to know how billionaires think, act, and invest to improve their careers, lifestyles, and fortunes.

Billionaires are powerful and influential. Many of them are captains of industry and highly respected business leaders. Money to them is an afterthought, as they're able to purchase extravagant items such as yachts, airplanes, mansions, and professional sports teams. Their lifestyles are unbelievable and not subject to the same daily hassles as everyone else. They can afford royal treatment and help at their beck and call. They're A-listers, privy and exposed to experiences that most people will never know or comprehend. Make no mistake, being a millionaire is not that same as being a billionaire. Billionaires are an anomalous breed unto themselves. However, not everyone is content with these wealthy elites, given their large sums of money and sway.

A sizable portion of the public has a negative view of billionaires and capitalism since the rich are only getting richer. Also, inequality and social mobility are ongoing hot topics globally. The world's richest people ended 2016 with $237 billion more than they had at the start of the year. Oxfam reported that the eight richest billionaires have as much wealth as the bottom half of the world's population. Eight is shocking considering the number was at sixty-two the previous year and 388 just a few years ago. Credit Suisse reports that just <u>0.7 percent</u> of the world's adult population owns almost half of the world's wealth, while the bottom 73 percent have less than $10,000 each. Affluent individuals and corporations are <u>cleverly using</u> tax laws, shelters, and havens to avoid paying taxes and their fair share. For example, Apple Inc. uses complex accounting strategies to <u>avoid paying taxes</u> on its cash hoard of over $250 billion. Furthermore, billionaires have attracted undesirable attention for their involvement in politics. In many countries, government officials and the super-rich are far too often seen mingling and rubbing shoulders. One must consider and be concerned with an ever-skewing distribution of wealth and power flowing into the hands of a few and how that money is being used. For example, launched by billionaires, the Giving Pledge is a worthy charitable initiative that benefits millions of people.

Whether your view of billionaires is positive or negative, they have taught us and can teach us a lot about business, career, wealth, personal transformation, and lifestyle. Bill Gates has proven that through entrepreneurship, a person can build both a successful software enterprise and a charitable foundation that seeks to eradicate the world's worst diseases. Richard Branson has shown that business can be serious, amusing, and enjoyable all at the same time. J. K. Rowling has demonstrated that writing imaginary tales about wizards and dragons can inspire as well as be hugely profitable. Warren Buffett has shown that being rich isn't necessarily about buying grandiose objects; he's owned the same <u>nonchalant house</u> he bought in the 1950s. Many billionaires have demonstrated an amazing tenacity to transform themselves from rags to riches, including Howard Schultz, Li Ka-shing, and Oprah Winfrey.

There are thousands of how-to and habit books that address wealth creation, and I've read many of them. Some have offered useful ideas while others received failing grades. A couple of popular books conducted thorough interviews with millionaires, and they outlined principles, behaviors, and financial planning activities worthy of emulating. These books, while substantive, limited their focus to mind-sets and behaviors of wealthy Americans without considering other factors that influence financial success. For example, these books didn't investigate issues such as gender and race, yet the richest self-made Americans are mostly male and white. These books didn't discuss the careers and incomes of women and nonwhites in America and elsewhere, and the challenges they face to become affluent. Wealth impacts everyone, so, our research accounts for cross-section of individuals.

This book is about self-made affluent individuals, particularly billionaires, in America and abroad, since we can learn as much from a Chinese billionaire as we can from an American one. Our aim was to uncover factors that are instrumental to wealth creation, beyond what is commonly known. For instance, it's widely accepted that living below your means can lead to achieving financial success. We've chosen not to focus on billionaires by inheritance because there's nothing fascinating about winning the family lottery or being born on third base—for example, being born a Walton, Hilton, or Johnson heir. If becoming a billionaire or millionaire is not your focus, don't worry. The factors we present impact everyone regardless of their income, net worth, and financial goals.

After reading this book, you'll understand the key issues that influence wealth accumulation. Furthermore, you'll be able to apply these concepts to improve your career, finances, and lifestyle. Whether the odds are in your favor or not, your willingness, commitment, and courage will ultimately influence your results.

THE SEVEN FACTORS

Who becomes a billionaire? Given there are approximately two thousand of them, very few individuals do. Billionaires and millionaires thrive in countries that encourage economic freedom, ease of doing business, and favorable free market principles. White males have largely been the demographic group most successful in becoming billionaires because they've been on the right side of history and privilege regarding power and control. People who possess the right career aspirations and personal traits fill the billionaire ranks. Birth year can be relevant in the accumulation of fortunes, depending on the surrounding environment. Lastly, there's an X factor—a unique circumstance, event, quality, or person that has had a strong but unpredictable influence on each billionaire. For instance, after being rejected by Harvard University, Warren Buffett enrolled at Columbia to hone his investment knowledge under the instruction of Benjamin Graham, the "father of value investing." Billionaires may experience one or multiple X factors, and identifying them is subject to debate. The seven factors that determine wealth include:

1. Residing country
2. Gender
3. Race, ethnicity, and skin color
4. Career aspirations
5. Personality traits
6. Birth year
7. X factor (a factor or factors unique to each billionaire)

RESEARCH

Billionaires are not exactly a phone call away, so my team and I based our research on thorough examination of more than eight-hundred articles from various leading sources. Thanks to intense competition regarding billionaire rankings, a lot of useful and insightful information is easily accessible. Articles from *Forbes*, *Fortune*, *Business Insider*, *Bloomberg*, and *The Wall Street Journal* were frequently referenced. We reviewed data from global institutions such as the United Nations, World Economic Forum, and World Bank, and we looked at think tanks such as the Heritage Foundation. Lastly, we found reports from Wealth-X and UBS to be valuable.

1 | Residing Country: Fertile Ground or Toxic Dump?

Becoming a billionaire is an exceptional achievement, and amassing astounding prosperity isn't a random occurrence. The accumulation of riches is based on a set of factors that, when present, enable individuals to create significant wealth. These factors tend to work in tandem so that no one factor is entirely responsible for fortunes made. Conversely, when these factors are not present, people will likely experience fewer, if any, opportunities to become affluent.

The seven factors influencing billionaire prospects are:

1. Residing country
2. Gender
3. Race, ethnicity, and skin color
4. Career aspirations
5. Personality traits
6. Birth year
7. X factor

Residing Country: Fertile Ground or Toxic Dump

Billionaire prospects begin with the country a person resides in, given he or she can access gainful employment. The profile and demographics of a country as they relate to economics, ease of doing business, human development, and so on influence the other six decisive factors. For instance, in a country with a command economy, career aspirations and personality traits are suppressed since the government is in full control of market activities. A brief comparison between North and South Korea highlights the importance of residing country.

Countries with the most billionaires (as of 2016):

Forbes	Wealth-X
United States -540	United States - 585
China - 251	China - 260
Germany - 120	Germany - 130
India - 84	Russia - 118
Russia - 77	United Kingdom - 106

North Korea is under totalitarian communist rule. They operate a command economy, which is where the state owns and controls almost all means of production and development. Economic freedoms are suppressed, and social mobility is virtually nonexistent through a rigid and antiquated caste system. The only person thought to be a billionaire is North Korea's "supreme leader," Kim Jong-un.

Given North Korea's economic and political climate, its residents can't fully engage in business activities that could make them wealthy even if they had promising aspirations and personality traits. Step across the border into South Korea, and you'll find an entirely different story.

South Korea is a highly technological, leading world economy that has given rise to global corporations, including Samsung Electronics, Hyundai Motors, and LG. They embrace democracy and operate a mixed economy infused with capitalist and socialist ideals. They support economic freedom and ease of doing business.

South Koreans can freely pursue business ventures locally and abroad. Career, lifestyle, and financial opportunities are vastly different for someone living and working in South Korea compared with their northern neighbor. There are thirty-one South Korean billionaires versus North Korea's one.

To appreciate residing country as a critical factor in the wealth-creation process, we need to understand various aspects, including these:

1. Economic systems
2. Economic prospects
3. Economic freedom
4. Ease of doing business
5. Social and economic mobility
6. Human development
7. Political structure
8. Population size
9. Entrepreneurial culture

ECONOMIC SYSTEMS

While true free market economies do not exist, many mixed economies enable individuals to pursue their business and economic interests freely. The countries with the most billionaires operate mixed economies. One example is Germany. In contrast, command economies limit people's economic choices. It's virtually impossible to become a billionaire in a state-controlled economy because of the stranglehold government has on industries and market activities. One example is Cuba.

A mixed economy is a blend of capitalism, where a majority of industries are privately owned, and socialism, where a minority of public utilities and essential services are controlled by government. Capitalism and free market attributes must be present to increase personal wealth. Individuals are incentivized to start businesses and offer goods and services that people want. Firms that successfully respond to the needs of consumers get rewarded with sales, profits, and higher valuations. Owners, key stakeholders, and investors get rich in the process.

Capitalism invites relatively low levels of government intervention, strong private property rights, economic freedom, ease of doing business, and low barriers to trade. Also, the market determines prices through the laws of supply and demand. The socialist aspect of a mixed economy calls for the government to own and control vital industries. Furthermore, the government regulates the output and pricing of these industries. For instance, Canadian Crown corporations are enterprises owned by the government of Canada. Those include the Royal Canadian Mint, which produces Canada's circulated coins, and Via Rail, which offers intercity passenger rail services.

Many Western countries have embraced a mix of capitalism and socialism, which has been advantageous for creating fortunes. America has led the way in producing billionaires through its support of free enterprise. Russia ushered in its first wave of billionaires in the 1990s when it went from a command economy to a mixed economy. China's transition to a mixed economy has had the same positive impact on individual wealth creation.

Each economic system has advantages and disadvantages and promoters and detractors. For example, capitalism isn't about everyone winning. Rather, the system creates winners (the rich), losers (the poor), and the potential for inequality. Bill Gates "won" because he demolished his competitors and got millions of people to purchase Microsoft's products. For Gates to have won, others had to have lost in varying degrees—like an Olympic competition with first, second, third, and subsequent places. Nevertheless, affluent individuals cannot emerge without the presence of capitalism.

ECONOMIC PROSPECTS

It takes a growing and expanding economy to create prosperity, whereas a stagnant or contracting economy tends to do the opposite. Economic growth equates to an increase in real gross domestic product. An increase in real GDP means there is a rise in the value of national output/expenditure. When an economy is growing, unemployment rates decrease. As more and more individuals gain employment, they attract higher incomes that enable them to enjoy more goods and services sold by businesses (businesses expand in the process). Governments borrow less for programs such as unemployment benefits due to increased revenue from wage and sales taxes. Finally, economic growth attracts domestic and foreign investment, which can lead to even more growth.

In a contracting economy, a downward spiral of activities takes place. GDP diminishes, businesses cease to expand, incomes stagnate or decrease, the rate of unemployment rises, and demand for goods and services declines.

It's much more difficult to sustain sales and profits and accumulate wealth in a gloomy economic environment. For instance, consider the impact the Great Recession had on Americans. US household wealth eventually fell by over $16 trillion from the peak of household wealth in the spring of 2007, which by some measurements was about six months before the start of the recession. Trillions of dollars were lost due to declines in real estate and investment values. In the months after the recession, the unemployment rate peaked at 10 percent, which was the highest since 1982. In times of economic contraction, generating profits and issuing paychecks can quickly turn to losses and downsizing.

Americans have been privy to decades of impressive economic growth, and their stock market indices have continued to achieve new highs. For example, the Dow Jones, S&P 500, and Nasdaq indices all reached historical highs in 2016. That stock markets and individual securities perform well is important in measuring billionaires' wealth because many billionaire valuations are tied to publicly traded securities. For example, to estimate the net worth of Oracle CEO Larry Ellison, the share price of software company Oracle would be a major consideration. Like any country, the United States has experienced multiple crashes and downturns, but its ability to forge ahead has kept opportunities and prosperity afloat. On the other hand, Japan's problematic economy continues to hamper growth and wealth creation.

Japan is the third-largest economy in the world and home to thirty-seven billionaires (as of February 17, 2017). The country experienced impressive GDP growth from the 1960s to the late 1980s. Its most watched stock market index, the Nikkei, peaked at 38,916 on December 29, 1989. Three years later, Japan's economy took a turn for the worse with a crash in real estate and stock market prices. Since the early '90s, Japan's economy has attracted low growth, deflation, negative interest rates, and large national debt. The Nikkei trades at less than half its value of twenty-five years ago. Given Japan's ongoing economic woes and unimpressive stock market performance, it's been less fertile ground for aspiring billionaires compared with the United States.

ECONOMIC FREEDOM

Economic freedom is nonexistent in North Korea and Cuba, and it is virtually absent in other countries where oppressive governments are present. In these countries, people's rights and opportunities to build wealth are severely hampered. Consequently, billionaires tend not to surface from these nations and under these government regimes. In contrast, countries that promote and support economic liberty yield wealthy individuals.

The *Index of Economic Freedom* is an annual guide published by the *Wall Street Journal* and The Heritage Foundation. The Heritage Foundation states, "Economic freedom is the fundamental right of every human to control his or her own labor and property. In an economically free society, individuals are free to work, produce, consume, and invest in any way they please. In economically free societies, governments allow labor, capital, and goods to move freely, and refrain from coercion or constraint of liberty beyond the extent necessary to protect and maintain liberty itself."

Measurement of economic freedom is made up of ten quantitative and qualitative factors that are grouped into four broad categories:

1. Rule of law—property rights and freedom from corruption
2. Limited government—fiscal freedom and government spending
3. Regulatory efficiency—business freedom, labor freedom, and monetary freedom
4. Open Markets—trade freedom, investment freedom, and financial freedom

The *Index of Economic Freedom* highlights the benefits of economic freedom by stating, "The ideals of economic freedom are strongly associated with healthier societies, cleaner environments, greater per capita wealth, human development, democracy, and poverty elimination... Economies rated 'free' or 'mostly free' enjoy incomes that are over twice the average levels in all other countries and more than four times higher than the incomes of 'repressed' economies. Nations with higher degrees of economic freedom prosper because they capitalize more fully on the ability of the free-market system to generate and reinforce dynamic growth through efficient resource allocation, value creation, and innovation."

Countries such as the United States, Germany, the UK, and Canada are rated "mostly free." Billionaires have been able to flourish in these economies given the rights and options they have regarding business dealings. Conversely, it's difficult to make financial progress if your economic freedoms and rights are limited, government and regulatory bodies are inefficient and controlling, and access to trade, capital, and markets is severely restricted.

Despite the impressive billionaire yields of Brazil, Russia, India, and China (also known as BRIC), these countries are rated "mostly unfree." Their rating suggest that billionaires have surfaced because of other economic conditions. For instance, they have had robust economic growth and shifting economic policies that favor capitalism.

EASE OF DOING BUSINESS

The World Bank Group publishes the ease of doing business index. It's a study of laws and regulations with input from more than ninety-six hundred government officials, lawyers, business consultants, accountants, and other professionals from 185 economies. Those professionals routinely advise on legal and regulatory requirements.

The *Doing Business* report is meant to measure regulations directly affecting businesses, and it does not directly measure more general conditions such as a nation's proximity to large markets, quality of infrastructure, inflation, or crime. A nation's ranking is based on an average of ten indicators:

1. Starting a business—procedures, time, cost, and the minimum capital required to open a new business
2. Dealing with construction permits—procedures, time, and cost to build a warehouse
3. Getting electricity—procedures, time, and cost required for a business to obtain a permanent electricity connection for a newly constructed warehouse
4. Registering property—Procedures, time, and cost to register commercial real estate
5. Getting credit—strength of legal rights index, depth of credit information index
6. Protecting investors—indices on the extent of disclosure, extent of director liability, and ease of shareholder lawsuits

7. Paying taxes—number of taxes paid, hours per year spent preparing tax returns, and total tax payable as a share of gross profit
8. Trading across borders—number of documents, cost, and time necessary to export and import
9. Enforcing contracts—procedures, time, and cost to enforce a debt contract
10. Resolving insolvency—the time, cost, and recovery rate (in percentage terms) under a bankruptcy proceeding

The index has received both praise and criticism. However, it does illustrate a positive correlation between ease of doing business and billionaire yield. If conducting business is easy, individuals gain opportunities to prosper. Countries with strong rankings provide favorable climates for new business pursuits. For example, credit is available to business owners, which is often a major obstacle for individuals who don't have enough capital to start or keep their businesses operating. The BRIC countries have mixed results in the index, so other economic factors need to be considered.

Countries that rank poorly are saddled with many obstacles, onerous procedures, high operating costs, poor investor protection, and so on regarding business activities. These setbacks and hurdles hamper people's ability to prosper financially. For instance, Haiti is ranked 181 of 190 countries, which suggests that business dealings aren't easy at all. Haiti's business environment lags Western countries significantly. For instance, it takes twelve steps and up to 140 days to start a business there, compared with six steps and up to seven days in the United States. The path to starting a business, and pursuit of profits, is extremely short in the United States compared to Haiti.

SOCIAL AND ECONOMIC MOBILITY

Rags-to-riches stories give everyone hope. Tales of how an underdog beats the odds to become a billionaire are inspirational. One is the story of Amancio Ortega, one world's richest people and founder of Zara. Born in 1936 to a railroad worker and housewife in northwestern Spain, Ortega started working in a clothing shop at age thirteen. In 1963, he started making women's bathrobes with his siblings and wife-to-be. The first Zara store opened in 1975, and from rags to billions he went.

Ortega's story is hardly the norm; that's the reason underdog-to-victor anecdotes capture our imaginations. Anyone can make financial progress, but for every Ortega, or Ikea founder Ingvar Kamprad, or casino magnate Sheldon Adelson, there are millions of people who don't overcome their humble beginnings. More likely are the stories of Bill Gates, Warren Buffett, and Donald Trump—individuals who leveraged their favorable starts in life to become super rich. Nevertheless, billionaires are byproducts of countries that offer social and economic mobility.

Social, economic, and socioeconomic mobility is the movement of individuals, families, households, or other categories of people within or between social classes in a society. It's a change in social status or economic level in comparison with others within a given location. Economic mobility allows people from humble beginnings to better their lifestyles and financial circumstances. Social mobility partly explains why individuals such as Sheldon Adelson and oil and gas businessman Harold Hamm became billionaires despite starting off extremely poor.

Some countries offer high degrees of social mobility—for example, the United States, Denmark, Canada, and Australia—while others offer far less or none—for example, North Korea, Cuba, Russia, and India. Furthermore, when economic freedom is present, it works in tandem with social mobility.

A person can be born poor in an industrialized country and become a billionaire with the right career aspirations and personality traits. Rags-to-riches stories are present in countries such as the United States, Spain, and Italy. Conversely, rags-to-riches stories are difficult to find where social mobility is hampered by an oppressive government or caste system, as is the case in North Korea and India, for instance.

In addition to its communist government, North Korea has a strict social classification system referred to as songbun. Songbun determines, among other things, where North Koreans can live, work, and what kind of education they can receive. Citizens are divided into five groups (from best to worst): special, nucleus, basic, complex, and hostile. Special status is rarely obtained, and nucleus is the standard. Basic status can lead to slight discrimination, and people deemed complex or hostile face considerable prejudice. If your songbun isn't good enough, you cannot do the following:

- Live in Pyongyang, the capital city
- Enter a good university, no matter how smart you are
- Be employed as a teacher or police officer

Songbun derives from two factors: the social position and actions of one's paternal ancestors and one's current career—for example, a worker, farmer, military man, teacher, or policeman. Since songbun partly stems from ancestry, it is virtually impossible to change since historical family records are kept in multiple locations. Thus, social mobility in North Korea is essentially preordained and extremely rigid.

India has produced its fair share of billionaires and ranks in the top five globally despite its social stratification system, which has premodern origins.

India's caste system is among the world's oldest forms of social stratification. The system is a social structure that divides different groups into ranked categories. Members of "higher" castes have greater social privileges than individuals of "lower" castes. The system divides Hindus into groups based on their karma (work) and dharma (duty). The system has given many rights to the upper castes, and it has, in turn, limited the privileges of other groups. It remained virtually unchanged for centuries, trapping people into fixed social orders from which it was impossible to escape.

- Brahmin—priests and teachers
- Kshatriya—rulers and warriors
- Vaishya—farmers, traders, and merchants
- Shudra—laborers
- Dalit (also known as "untouchables")—street sweepers and cleaners

Job quotas in government and academia were set in the 1950s to correct historical injustices and level the playing field. Although Indian law prohibits discrimination by caste, discrimination is still present, which greatly limits social mobility for some groups. The Dalits, members of India's most oppressed group, continue to protest for economic mobility.

Oprah Winfrey's mother was a maid, and Harold Hamm's parents were sharecroppers. In America, Winfrey and Hamm rose to prominence, but in North Korea and India, their prospects would have been far more limited under their respective caste systems.

DEVELOPED COUNTRIES COMPARED

Social mobility isn't just opportune for individuals born into lower classes; it's advantageous for anyone who wants to improve his or her livelihood and well-being. While economic mobility is present in many developed countries, the degree to which it differs highlights the importance of location.

The State of Working America, 12th Edition, measures the relationship between earnings of fathers and sons in OECD member countries and the United States. An elasticity of zero would mean there is no relationship—with poor children having as much chance as rich children to end up as rich adults. The higher the elasticity, the greater chance that parental earnings affect the incomes of their children.

The elasticity rating between father-son earnings is higher in the United States than in most OECD countries, suggesting low social mobility. For example, with an elasticity of 0.47, the United States offers much less social mobility than Canada, Finland, Norway, and Denmark.

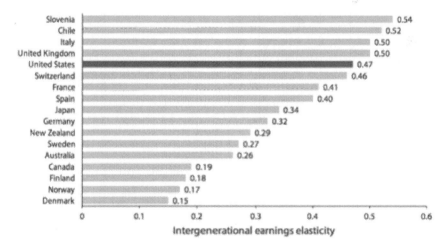

Note: The higher the intergenerational elasticity, the lower the extent of mobility.

Source: Economic Policy Institute

SOCIAL CLASS IN AMERICA

Social mobility in America may not be as high compared with other countries or compared with what it <u>once was</u>, but it's present nonetheless. If social mobility is as forgiving as one might think, then the class a person is born into shouldn't have dire consequences. However, research shows the opposite. Although America doesn't have a caste system, it's social class stratification highly influences how well individuals do financially over the long term.

Social class refers to a group of people with similar levels of wealth, influence, and status. There are various models and definitions regarding social classes, but we can look to these definitions for a general understanding:

- The upper-upper class includes aristocratic and "high-society" families with "old money" who have been rich for generations.
- The lower-upper class includes those with "new money," or money made from investments and business ventures.
- The upper-middle class is made up of highly educated professionals with high incomes, such as doctors, lawyers, accountants, and executives.
- The lower-middle class consists of less educated people with lower incomes, such as managers, small business owners, and secretaries.
- The lower class is typified by poverty, homelessness, inadequate education, criminal behavior, and unemployment.

The working class is made up of those with minimal education who engage in manual labor with little or no prestige. Unskilled workers in the class—dishwashers, cashiers, maids, and waitresses—are usually underpaid and have little opportunity for career advancement. They are considered the "working poor." Skilled workers in this class—carpenters, plumbers, and electricians—are considered blue-collar workers. They may make more money than workers in the middle class—secretaries, teachers, and computer technicians; however, their jobs are usually more physically taxing, and in some cases quite dangerous.

The three-stratum model of social classes condenses groups into three general categories: a very wealthy and powerful upper class that owns and controls the means of production; a middle class of professional workers, small business owners, and low-level managers; and a lower class, who rely on low-paying wage jobs.

Using the three-stratum model while considering subclasses, we researched the early lives and backgrounds of the forty American billionaires in the top one hundred. We stuck to American billionaires since concrete biographical information is readily available compared with billionaires from other countries. Where parents were professionals—such as doctors, lawyers, dentists or psychiatrists (as is the case with Facebook CEO Mark Zuckerberg, the son of a dentist and psychiatrist)—we grouped these individuals into the upper class.

Sixty-five percent (26/40) of the richest American billionaires were born into upper-class families, 28 percent (11/40) were born into middle-class families, and 7 percent (3/40) into lower-class families.

It's obvious that most of the wealthiest Americans were born to upper- and middle-class families, which impacted their eventual success. For instance, Bill Gates was born to successful and established parents; his father was a lawyer, and his mother was the president of the local United Way. Warren Buffett's dad was a stockbroker turned congressman. Larry Page and Sergey Brin were born to university professors and researchers. Thomas Frist's father was a prominent physician and businessman. These examples tend to be commonplace compared with billionaires who beat the odds and speak to the importance of nurture in the ongoing nature vs. nurture debate. Also, what's noticeable about ultrawealthy billionaires is that many of them had parents who were professionals, educators, and entrepreneurs in tandem with their middle- and upper-class upbringings.

There are advantages and disadvantages associated with social classes that affect the probability of becoming wealthy. A person born to an affluent family can expect to do the following:

- Live in a safe home and neighborhood
- Attain an excellent education
- Eat nutritious food and have access to outstanding health care
- Live longer than poor people
- Gain favorable entrance into colleges and companies
- Leverage family creditworthiness, access capital, and perhaps gain contacts for business and professional ventures

Some wealthy parents (and relatives) go as far as to buy (bribe) their way into top universities, on behalf of their children, by making large donations or alternative transactions. These actions make it harder for high-achieving students from lower-class families to get into excellent schools because enrollment is often limited.

Although start-up funding is more accessible than ever and can be obtained through several different methods, being able to tap family members for financial assistance can be much more advantageous for potential billionaires. For instance, family dealings may allow for better ownership terms compared with those requested by venture capitalists and outside investors.

Donald Trump is a fantastic example of someone who benefited from family capital. According to Trump, "It has not been easy for me. And you know, I started off in Brooklyn, my father gave me a small loan of a million dollars." In fact, Trump received additional loans and gifts to assist his business activities. In contrast, low-income families can ill afford to provide their children with financial resources or "small loans."

Children from low-income families don't have the same luxuries as rich ones. They may be exposed to increased domestic violence and neighborhood crime. The schools they go to may be poorly funded compared with the private schools that rich children attend. Moreover, poor children may be forced to drop out to help their families make ends meet. The odds of being born poor and becoming a billionaire are extremely low compared with the odds for those who are born on third base. Research shows that wealthy Americans were more than eight times more likely to graduate from college than lower-income Americans. Poor neighborhoods are more susceptible to higher obesity rates, which curtail life expectancies. If we shift the discussion to becoming a millionaire, Author Thomas Stanley reports, "Children of affluent parents have (in today's dollars) about a one-in-five chance of accumulating wealth in the seven figures during their lifetimes, while the average child in this country whose parents are not millionaires has about a one-in-thirty chance." (*The Millionaire Next Door*, p. 160.)

As Dr. Tian Dayton puts it, "It is no social secret that having wealth can provide a person with status, power, and open the doors to acquiring education and polish." Bill Gates and Warren Buffett didn't have to experience the rough-and-tumble environments that lower-class children often endure. Gates was privileged to have access to elite schools and computer systems while never having to worry about basic survival. And Buffett could participate in business ventures and investing without worrying about getting shot on the way home. Furthermore, many children from prosperous backgrounds have the luxury of time—they have more time to focus on their work if maids and helpers are present.

All the advantages associated with upper classes dramatically increase the chances of becoming affluent. It's like being born at different starting lines. Imagine for a moment that you're about to run the one hundred-meter dash. You are told to begin at the regular starting line while your opponent gets to start five meters from the finish line. There's a chance you may beat your opponent if he falls or decides to quit before crossing the finish line, but 90 percent of the time he's going to beat you because of his head start. People who are born into slavery and debt start way back in the pack.

95 to 97 percent of people start here.   2 to 4 percent of people start here.   1 percent of people or "family lottery winners" start here.

Starting line   100-Meter financial dash   Finish line / financial success

In a well-written piece, Chuck Collins, author of *Born on Third Base*, says, "The culprit is the growing role of inherited advantage, as affluent families make investments that give their children a leg up… We are witnessing accelerating advantages for the wealthy and compounding disadvantages for everyone else. A key determinant in these diverging prospects is the role of family wealth, a factor that plays an oversize role in sorting today's coming-of-age generation onto different opportunity trajectories. The initial sort begins much earlier. A growing mountain of research chronicles what sociologists call the 'intergenerational transmission of advantage,' including the myriad mechanisms by which affluent families boost their children's prospects starting at birth. The mechanisms include financial investments in their children's enrichment, school readiness, formal schooling, college access, and aiding the transition to work.

Meanwhile, the children in families unable to make these investments fall further behind."

Gregory Clark, author of *The Son Also Rises: Surnames and the History of Social Mobility*, suggests, "With surprising consistency across countries and eras, mobility is found to be painfully slow. Birth has predicted more than 50% of one's income or education status. Erasing the legacy of past prosperity takes 10–15 generations rather than the three or four implied by sunnier estimates. So, the shadow of 18th-century wealth still darkens income distributions today."

One study after another confirms that social mobility is more of an American dream and less of a reality if you start from the bottom rungs. A couple of studies by Pew Research Center further support this argument. A study on parental income shows a robust correlation between the amount of money one makes as a byproduct of how much money one's parents made. A different study shows that people born into lower-income households have low chances of rising into the middle- and upper-class income brackets.

Social mobility is also being hindered by income inequality. It's difficult to experience upward mobility if your income and financial resources aren't making significant gains. Research published by the Washington Center for Equitable Growth shows incomes for the top 1 percent of Americans increased from $990,000 in 2009 to $1,360,000 in 2015, a growth of 37 percent. The bottom 99 percent experienced gains of 7.6 percent during the same period, reaching an average income of $48,800. Emmanuel Saez, author of the report, says, "Income inequality in the United States persists at extremely high levels, particularly at the very top of the income ladder."

The rich are getting richer, which allows them to create more opportunities for themselves while everyone else experiences fewer economic prospects due to paltry income growth. As Collins says, "This race of accelerating advantages and compounding disadvantages is a disturbingly accurate metaphor for inherited privilege. Among 'high achievers,' the top 4 percent of students nationwide, 34 percent come from the top quartile, households with incomes of more than $120,776. Only 17 percent come from the bottom quartile, with incomes of less than $41,472. The income-achievement gap is now bigger than the race gap, a reverse from 50 years earlier. The main explanation is that high-income parents of all races are investing more in children's cognitive development."

Economic mobility is location dependent. In the United States, economists find that "the probability of a child born into the poorest fifth of the population in San Jose, California, making it to the top is 12.9%, not much lower than in Denmark. In Charlotte, North Carolina, it is 4.4%, far lower than anywhere else in the rich world." The economists cite five factors that influence social mobility, including residential segregation, the quality of schooling, family structure, social capital, and inequality. For example, those economists say, "Social mobility is higher in integrated places with good schools, strong families, lots of community spirit and smaller income gaps within the broad middle class."

Every nation has its set of issues regarding social and economic mobility, but a country that supports economic freedom and social progress provides everyone with a chance to improve his or her lot in life. Billionaires depend on masses of people to make their fortunes. If a healthy dose of social mobility is present, then people will be able to afford improvements to their lives in the form of products and services. For example, increased social mobility in China has led to more and more Chinese billionaires.

HUMAN DEVELOPMENT FACTORS

America is a developed country with a highly advanced economy and technological infrastructure. For decades, the United States has been one of the best places to live in terms of human development, which includes vital factors such as life expectancy, education, and per capita income. When you have a population as large as America's—with hundreds of millions of educated people who are expected to live long and who have money to spend—it creates an environment for billionaires to thrive. In contrast, the Philippines is a developing country. As a developing country, health, education, and poverty remain major challenges that negatively impact millions of Filipinos. The Philippines is categorized as "medium" to America's "very high" in the UN's Human Development Index (HDI) rankings. Countries with unfavorable HDI rankings tend to have very few billionaires, if any. For instance, Niger has no billionaires.

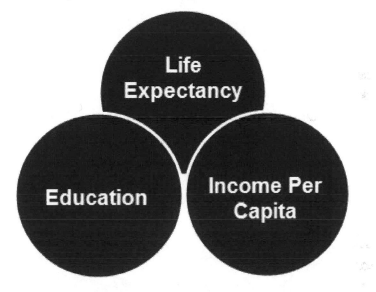

One major factor in the UN's Human Development Index is a long life expectancy. It suggest that a country's quality of life is good because of satisfactory health, economic, political, and social programs. For example, most Americans can expect to live relatively long lives, and the same is true for people in Japan and many European countries. Citizens of these countries can easily access good health care, immunization treatment, sanitation, clean water, and good nutrition. Access to these things allows them to carry out long, productive careers because they can remain in good health. Americans, Canadians, Germans, and Singaporeans can live long and prosper. On the other hand, countries riddled with low life expectancies, poor health care, famine, and so on tend to produce low economic prospects and societies of poor people. Among them, for instance, are Somalia, Chad, Mozambique, and Malawi.

Today, we see many twenty-somethings become billionaires. For instance, there's Evan Spiegel of Snap Inc. However, many billionaires achieve significant wealth on the back end of their lives. For instance, Warren Buffett didn't become a billionaire until he was fifty-six. It usually takes a few decades to accumulate riches, with long life expectancies required.

Education is another major HDI factor. It is a major component of well-being and standard of living, and it's a measure of economic development in terms of whether a country is considered developed, developing, or underdeveloped. The United States is ranked fifth by the United Nations, which uses a formula of mean years of schooling and expected years of schooling. While America's educational system is far from perfect, it's robust enough to have made it a global economic power. Furthermore, the United States boasts many of the world's best colleges and universities, including Harvard, Columbia, Princeton, MIT, and Stanford. These same universities have played a role in making four of the top five billionaires, including Bill Gates, Warren Buffett, Jeff Bezos, and Mark Zuckerberg.

Human capital is another area of human development that influences lifestyle and economic prospects. It's the collection of resources—all the knowledge, talents, skills, experiences, intelligence, training, judgment, and wisdom—possessed individually and collectively as a population. The United States and many European countries are rich in human capital, and thus they rank well in this regard.

Being a nation of abundant human capital yields a society of highly educated and skilled workers who can attract gainful employment. Millions of knowledge workers—from software engineers to accountants—have been present in the United States, Germany, Japan, and so on, and they have stimulated economic growth, innovation, and individual prosperity. Conversely, countries where human capital has been low have struggled to make inroads regarding economic and human development.

The third critical facet of HDI is income per capita. It's a measure of the amount of money earned per person in a specific area—for example, a city, region, or country. It's calculated by dividing a country's national income by its population.

Relatively high per capita income supports an economy and environment where billionaires can prosper. If the average citizen is earning enough, he or she will pour some of his or her money back into the economy. On the other hand, a society of people who barely make enough to survive—for instance, societies in Burundi or Malawi—will have less disposable income to stimulate economic growth and financial prosperity for others.

POLITICAL SYSTEMS

Democratic countries frequently support free market activities, whereas communist countries often operate command and planned economies. While economic systems have greater implications for billionaires than political systems, political systems can substantially impact economic and wealth prospects. Political instability refers to government collapse either because of conflicts or rampant competition between various political parties. If a government is unsuccessful or unstable, this can have dire consequences. For instance, insufficient US government oversight and weak banking regulations led to the Great Recession and global financial meltdown of 2008 and 2009.

Where capitalism is present, governments can support wealth creation by doing the following:

1. Being efficient and pragmatic
2. Reducing government corruption and cronyism
3. Implementing robust regulatory institutions, laws, individual rights, and freedoms

4. Employing effective monetary and fiscal policies
5. Improving human development conditions
6. Creating and upholding friendly and probusiness environments

When good governance and stewardship can advance these six factors, individuals' chances of creating prosperity are improved. Economist Zahid Hussain says, "Irrespective of political regimes, if a country does not need to worry about conflicts and radical changes of regimes, then people can concentrate on working, saving, and investing... Not all forms of political stability are equally development friendly; much depends on the extent to which stability translates into good governance."

China is unique in that it blends authoritarianism and capitalism. Its government isn't entirely communist, but it's far from being fully democratic. Despite China's political rigidity, changes to their economic system has spurred individual wealth.

Before the second stage of China's economic reforms in the late 1980s and 1990s, many industries were still state-owned, economic freedom was limited, and price controls and heavy regulations were in place, making it resemble a command economy. It was the completion of China's reforms and adoption of free market principles that produced Chinese billionaires starting in the mid-2000s. Political philosophies may be slow to change, but capitalism has given rise to many millionaires and billionaires.

POPULATION SIZE

Making billions through product and service revenues is usually dependent on capturing millions of customers. For instance, it's unlikely that Leonardo Del Vecchio would have become a billionaire had he limited sales of his glasses and lens to just Italy. It was his desire to expand vertically and globally that propelled his fortunes.

Countries such as China, India, the United States, Indonesia, Brazil, and so on have very large populations. You can start a business in these countries and generate significant revenue without having to expand internationally. In contrast, trying to amass riches in a country such as Andorra would be problematic given its population size of eighty-five thousand people. People in Andorra, which is bordered by Spain and France, know that if they desire substantial fortunes, they have to expand beyond Andorra. Not surprisingly, a search for billionaires from Andorra drew blanks. The top twenty-five countries with the most billionaires all have a minimum of twenty million citizens except for four: Switzerland, Israel, Sweden, and Hong Kong, which is technically an administrative region of China.

We can better understand the role population plays in creating wealth by comparing the United States to Canada. America and Canada are both developed countries, with high literacy rates, mixed economies, democracies, and white majorities. Yet Canada has thirty-three billionaires to America's 540. The reason Canada has 94 percent fewer billionaires than America is partly due to the differences in population size.

The United States has a population of 324 million, and Canada has 36 million. All things equal, an individual who sells a product or service nationwide in the United States has nearly ten times the population to exploit before leaving its borders. The United States simply has a bigger economy and market compared with Canada's. (America's GDP was roughly twelve times bigger than Canada's as of 2015.) If you want to "make it big," you need a large market to support you, domestically or abroad.

Let's consider the entertainment industry for a moment. Entertainers from Australia and Canada can gain respectable work in their homelands. However, if they want to achieve global recognition, they must succeed in larger markets such as the United States and UK. For example, Canadian actors Jim Carrey and Jason

Priestley and singers Alanis Morissette and Justin Bieber became rich and famous only after they achieved stardom in America.

There are twelve countries with populations greater than one hundred million people (as of 2015), but none of them match or exceed the United States in billionaires. (China and India had roughly four times as many citizens as the United States as of 2016.) While a sizeable population can be beneficial to building wealth, in isolation it's not a critical factor. It's population size in combination with favorable economic factors that stimulate individual prosperity. For example, Indonesia is home to 255 million people, yet it has produced fewer than thirty billionaires. It has fewer billionaires than Canada, which has a population of 36 million. Canada offers much more favorable economic and human development conditions than Indonesia.

The Internet has accelerated globalization, and many e-commerce businesses have benefited in the process. Therefore, it's possible to reside in a country with average economic prospects and tap into another country with more favorable prospects without physically being present. What's more, an e-commerce company must achieve success in a country with a large population—or multiple countries with sizable populations—to generate significant revenues and wealth for its owner(s). For example, Australia has a robust economy but a relatively small population of roughly twenty-four million people. An Australian e-commerce company might expand to the United States to try to increase their revenues.

ENTREPRENEURIAL CULTURE

America has been highly proficient at creating billionaires since it produced the first one in John D. Rockefeller over one hundred years ago. It has long been viewed as the "land of opportunity" for people to chase "the American dream." The American dream is a national philosophy and set of ideals that promotes prosperity, success, and upward social mobility for everyone who works hard.

These ideals are rooted in the Declaration of Independence, which proclaims that "all men are created equal" with the right to "Life, Liberty and the pursuit of Happiness." This national ethos speaks to achieving lifestyle and career success whether a person climbs the corporate ladder or starts a business.

Americans have a lot of gumption and embody entrepreneurship just as much, if not more than, citizens of any other country. With "the land of opportunity" in mind, the United States is successful at creating a climate to cultivate entrepreneurs and self-made millionaires or billionaires.

The Global Entrepreneurship and Development Institute (The GEDI Institute) is a research organization that advances knowledge on links between entrepreneurship, economic development, and prosperity. Its main contribution is the Global Entrepreneurship Index (GEI), an annual index that measures the health of entrepreneurship in 137 countries. The GEI is composed of three subindices: entrepreneurial attitudes, entrepreneurial activity, and entrepreneurial aspirations. These subindices consist of fourteen pillars that contain individual and institutional variables that correspond to the micro- and macro-level aspects of entrepreneurship.

America ranks first, followed by other countries that have high billionaire tallies, including Switzerland, Canada, Australia, the UK, Germany, and France. Naturally, a culture and environment that welcomes capitalism, free enterprise, and entrepreneurship is one that can yield affluent individuals.

To support entrepreneurs, the United States offers a more robust and expansive network for venture capital investments than its peers. From 2006 to 2013, the United States was the largest recipient of investments globally. They totaled $255 billion. Europe was second, with $55 billion, followed by China, Israel, India, and Canada. Also, Ivy League and other top American universities have extremely large endowment funds that range in the billions of dollars. These same funds allocate capital to start-ups, which benefits American entrepreneurs and fortunate entrepreneurs abroad. For instance, Stanford invested and <u>profited</u> from Google's initial public offering, and it has held stakes in Sun Microsystems, Cisco Systems, and Yahoo.

WHERE TO LIVE

The country you reside in has a tremendous impact on your wealth prospects. If accumulating riches in your priority, then you'll want to live in a country with favorable economic systems, freedoms, social mobility, and human development indicators. Also, it should be easy to do business, government interference should be minimal, and a generous population size and entrepreneurial culture are advantageous. If you were born in such a country, you've won a lottery of sorts.

2 | GENDER: IT'S STILL A MAN'S WORLD, BUT WOMEN ARE RISING

Gender has played a significant role in the distribution and accumulation of wealth. Male privilege and the patriarchal system—a social system in which males hold primary power and predominate in roles of political leadership, moral authority, social privilege, and control of property—have benefited men for centuries. Males have dominated and still dominate positions of authority, from rulers to priests and from heads of state to corporate executives. The universe dealt women fewer rights, opportunities, and fortunes, but they have made inroads in the billionaire ranks, with some countries offering more opportunities than others.

The top one hundred self-made billionaires are all male, and there are 8.4 male billionaires for every female billionaire. Fewer than 7 percent of Fortune 1000 chief executives are women, and women account for about one in ten of today's leaders of United Nation member states. Pioneering tech companies like Facebook, Google, and Uber continue to report dismal statistics concerning women in senior and technical positions. American women are paid less than men for the same work, and the gap is worse for women of color. Sexism and gender prejudice is alive and well in the workplace with men enjoying a 30 percent more likelihood than women to be promoted from entry level to management. Women in professional sports such as tennis experience an enormous pay gap. When the government forced the British Broadcasting Corporation

(BBC) to <u>publish the salary ranges</u> of its highest-paid entertainers and journalists, it revealed a significant disparity in the salaries received by women compared with men. Only one-third of the BBC's top-paid stars are women. In Vatican City, only men can vote, and while Saudi Arabia has recently permitted women to vote, they're banned from driving there. These examples of inequality highlight how much men are favored to succeed in business, prosperity, and other aspects of daily life from top to bottom. In more traditional societies and communist countries, male privileges can be more excessive.

Male domination over the centuries produced compounding advantages for them while crippling prospects for women during the same period. Still, pioneering countries that have championed women's rights and gender equality—for instance, <u>Iceland and Norway</u>—have improved the treatment, conditions, opportunities, and perceptions of women. These are countries women should look to for promising wealth prospects. Also, women's presence in politics is becoming more commonplace. For instance, Angela Merkel is a German politician and Chancellor of Germany since 2005 while Theresa May has served as Prime Minister of the United Kingdom and Leader of the Conservative Party since July 2016.

Despite the barriers and glass ceilings that exist, it's easier to become a self-made female billionaire today than it was decades ago. The number of female billionaires grew by a <u>factor</u> of 6.6 from 1995 to 2014 compared with a factor of 5.2 for males. China is home to <u>two-thirds</u> of self-made female billionaires, with forty-nine, and the United States is second, with fifteen. From Zhou Qùnfei (China) to Kiran Mazumdar-Shaw (India) to Diane Hendricks (United States), female entrepreneurs and billionaires are rising and part of a new normal.

Some countries and companies are more welcoming and supportive than others concerning gender equality, entrepreneurship, and career advancement. Therefore, women have options if they desire greater equality and rights. There are multiple reports that highlight gender equality issues and statistics that can be used to make informed decisions about where to live and work. For example, the United Nations Development Programme's *Gender Inequality Index* and the Human Rights Campaign's *Corporate Equality Index* can help with such decisions.

3 | RACE, ETHNICITY, AND SKIN COLOR: MAJORITY RULES

America is a multicultural country with sizeable racial groups, including white, black, Latino, and Asian populations. Wealth among these groups is unequally distributed and not proportional. For example, black Americans are the second-largest racial group, at <u>13 percent</u>. With the recent addition of basketball legend Michael Jordan, there are only three black US billionaires. That equates to less than 1 percent of all American billionaires.

Whether you're a part of the majority or minority, you might be wondering why groups are overrepresented or underrepresented in positions of wealth, power, and control. Possessing the same skin color, race, ethnicity, or religion as those in prominent positions within a country greatly influences the chances of achieving prosperity.

The idea of "privilege" is that some people benefit from unearned, and largely unacknowledged, advantages, even when those advantages aren't discriminatory. In contrast, white privilege (or white skin privilege) is a term for societal privileges that benefit people identified as white in Western countries when those privileges are beyond what is commonly experienced by nonwhite people under the same social, political, or economic circumstances.

The concept of white privilege gained attention when Peggy McIntosh, a women's studies scholar, addressed it. In 1988, McIntosh wrote a paper called "White Privilege and Male Privilege:

A Personal Account of Coming to See Correspondences Through Work in Women's Studies," which contained forty-six examples of white privilege. For instance, it said, "I can go shopping alone most of the time, fairly well assured that I will not be followed or harassed by store detectives." Also, it said, "If a traffic cop pulls me over or if the IRS audits my tax return, I can be sure I haven't been singled out because of my race." According to McIntosh, "I have come to see white privilege as an invisible package of unearned assets that I can count on cashing in each day, but about which I was 'meant' to remain oblivious. White privilege is like an invisible weightless knapsack of special provisions, assurances, tools, maps, guides, codebooks, passports, visas, clothes, compass, emergency gear, and blank checks."

The relationship between white privilege, power, control, and wealth in Western countries is that white people attract more advantages than their nonwhite counterparts. Caucasians benefit from "unearned assets" and "special provisions" in various aspects of career and life, allowing them to accumulate greater riches than nonwhites. For instance, in American politics, white people, specifically white males, fill most critical positions. Additionally, white Americans gain the upper hand in other sectors, such as business, law, medicine, arts and entertainment, education, fashion, and so on. Since the balance of power remains with whites, they continue to benefit from white skin privilege. Some numbers provide some insights:

- Forty-four of forty-five US presidents have been white males.
- The median wealth of white households is thirteen times the median wealth of black households.
- White males outearn black and Hispanic men and all groups of women.
- White high school dropouts are wealthier than black and Hispanic college graduates.

44

- Whites represent approximately <u>91 percent</u> of Fortune 500 CEOs.
- <u>Poverty rates</u> in the United States are much lower for whites than for blacks and Hispanics.
- Job applicants with white-sounding names are <u>50 percent</u> more likely to get called back for an interview than similarly qualified applicants with black-sounding names.
- Black people, Latinos, and Native Americans are <u>underrepresented in tech</u> by 16 to 18 percentage points compared with their presence in the US labor force overall.
- Making matters worse, people of color in tech <u>report</u> experiencing discrimination, stereotyping, and unfair behavior or treatment, which is prompting many to leave the sector.

Not only does white privilege attract invisible and visible advantages, but nonwhites are intentionally and systematically <u>disadvantaged</u> in part because the majority—in any country—seeks to retain power, control, and wealth. The critically acclaimed documentary 13th highlights these points well.

For somebody to be richer, somebody must be poorer, which resembles the zero-sum game economic theory. Since the majority doesn't want to become poor or lose power, they attempt to suppress the minority by any means possible. For example, Jim Crow laws were state and local laws that enforced racial segregation in the Southern United States. As this <u>article states</u>, "In legal theory, blacks received "separate but equal" treatment under the law — in actuality, public facilities for blacks were nearly always inferior to those for whites, when they existed at all. In addition, blacks were systematically denied the right to vote in most of the rural South through the selective application of literacy tests and other racially motivated criteria."

Black and Hispanic Americans have been subject to bias from financial and criminal justice systems that unfairly discriminate and punish them compared with Caucasians. Decades of mistreatment of nonwhites has had a lasting negative impact on their socioeconomic prospects:

- <u>Black and Hispanic</u> business owners are less likely to be approved for business loans than whites.
- <u>Blacks and Hispanics</u> are more likely to attract discriminatory mortgage lending practices.
- <u>Jumbos loans</u> above $417,000 in most markets are granted to fewer blacks and Hispanics.
- <u>Blacks and Hispanics</u> have a 6 percent chance of becoming millionaires; that compares to a 22 percent probability for whites.
- <u>Black and Hispanic</u> motorists are more likely to be given tickets than white drivers stopped for the same offenses.
- <u>Black Americans</u> are more likely to serve longer sentences than white Americans for the same crimes.
- <u>Black and Hispanic</u> Americans are more likely to endure police brutality—like being roughly patted down, grabbed, handcuffed, struck with a baton, or pressed up against a wall—than whites.

White privilege is also noticeable in Europe. A <u>review</u> by the Equality and Human Rights Commission, Great Britain's national equality body, revealed the following:

- Black workers with degrees earn 23.1 percent less on average than white employees with the same qualifications.
- Unemployment rates were "significantly higher" for ethnic minorities.
- Ethnic minorities were more likely to live in poverty than white people.
- Ethnic minorities are still hugely underrepresented in positions of power—such as judges and police chiefs.

Other Western countries—such as Australia, Canada, France, Germany, and Italy—report similar findings to those above regarding whites and nonwhites, or "visible minorities." If we single out Canada, decades of white privilege have resulted in twenty-four of the top twenty-five richest Canadians being Caucasian. While Canada is considered very racially diverse, it's barely noticeable among the wealthiest Canadians.

A history of slavery, segregation, racism, and white privilege has not benefited nonwhites in Western countries. Conversely, whites dominate the wealth ranks, and of the top one hundred self-made billionaires, more than 60 percent are white males from Europe and the United States. Nonwhites in the top one hundred are from non-Western countries such as China and Japan.

You can be a foreign-born Caucasian male, immigrate to the United States, and have a better chance at becoming a billionaire than an American-born black or Hispanic. White, foreign-born US billionaires (twenty-plus) far outnumber black and Hispanic American-born billionaires combined (four, including Robert Smith, Oprah Winfrey, Michael Jordan, and Arte Moreno).

White privilege has a psychological impact on both whites and nonwhites. It's relatively easy for a white person to envision his success, given the accomplishments of so many others just like him. In contrast, nonwhites aren't exposed to the same breadth and depth of achievement. For example, it would be easier for a white Canadian to envision becoming the country's next prime minister (all twenty-three prime ministers have been white) than a Chinese-Canadian who doesn't have the equivalent reference point. The same idea applies to wealth and billionaire references. Furthermore, the psychological impact of white privilege can influence people's self-esteem and ambitions. Whites can feel more confident given Western societies' favoritism toward them.

MAJORITY PRIVILEGE

White privilege is present in Westernized countries; however, on a global level, it gives way to a more universal concept called "majority privilege." Majority privilege is a term for societal and economic advantages that are passed to people who resemble the majority in power within a country. There tends to be a trickle-down effect among the majority in control and those with similarities in race, skin color, ethnicity, religion, and gender. In contrast, if you don't resemble the mainstream, the odds of you becoming wealthy or a billionaire are reduced. For instance, Chinese citizens in China would have advantages over Korean and Japanese minorities, and Indians living in India would receive "assurances" over Pakistani and Bangladeshi minorities. Along the same lines, a Chinese person living in Russia or Peru is bound to experience fewer privileges than the majorities of those respective countries. The correlation between those in power and wealth isn't 100 percent, but billionaires are likely to resemble the majority in control, with Western countries yielding Caucasian billionaires and Asian countries producing Asian billionaires.

There are many wealthy blacks in Africa, where majority privilege benefits them, which is the opposite of what they experience in Western countries. White billionaires also make South Africa's rich list because of runoff from once being in control through apartheid. Apartheid was a former policy of social, political, and economic guidelines that systematically discriminated against non-European groups. When white South Africans were in power, financial conditions and opportunities overwhelmingly benefited them. When apartheid ended, black South Africans could claim prominent positions and make inroads. For instance, Nelson Mandela was freed from prison and became the country's first black head of state.

What can be said about government positions (power) and their correlation to billionaires (wealth)? China's parliament consists mainly of Chinese nationals at a ratio of three males to one female.

48

At the same time, with roughly two hundred and fifty Chinese billionaires, Chinese males dominate the list. India's government is male-centric, at <u>88 percent</u> of parliamentary positions, and of its eighty-four billionaires, eighty or 95 percent are men. Government demographics often resemble the demographics of wealthy individuals.

It's important to note that greater female representation within a country's political framework doesn't necessarily correlate to output of female billionaires. Gender, not race, is the hurdle that women face. For instance, females represent <u>40 percent</u> of Spain's parliament, but of the country's twenty-one billionaires, only five females (24 percent) make the list. (Only two of the five are self-made.)

Given that majorities experience advantages over minorities, why would minorities stay in or move to a country that doesn't favor them? Minorities may stay for any number of reasons, such as convenience, relationships, financial ties, relocation challenges, or lack of appealing alternatives. As for emigrants, accumulating riches may not be their top priority. Individuals relocate for other reasons—for instance, to experience a better way of life, career prospects, relationships, safety, and economic and political stability. For example, refugees may be forced to leave their countries to escape war, persecution, or natural disaster.

Many governments have enacted reverse discrimination policies to favor members of disadvantaged groups that currently suffer or historically have suffered from bias within a country. These policies seek to bridge inequalities in employment and pay, increase access to education, promote diversity, and address past wrongs, harms, and hindrances. For example, minorities might receive preference or special consideration in employment selection processes. Consequently, it's possible for minorities to benefit from positive discrimination to partially offset majority privileges; otherwise, minorities lose out to majorities.

A BRIEF NOTE ABOUT HEIGHT

Like skin color, height is a physical attribute. There are plenty of studies that highlight the relationship between people's heights and how much they earn. Taller people on average earn more than shorter people. However, height impacts employees more than entrepreneurs. For example, Facebook co-founder Mark Zuckerberg is five feet seven inches (5'7'), which is considered short by American and European standards. A company seeking to fill a customer-facing position may pass on Zuckerberg, or someone short, irrespective of his qualifications. On the other hand, as an entrepreneur and co-founder, Zuckerberg circumvents discriminatory hiring practices.

On a positive note, the more promising a person's business idea is, the less other people—like investors—care about that person's physical attributes.

4 | Career Aspirations: The Entrepreneurial Shift

Pursuing millions or billions of dollars isn't for everyone and especially not for individuals who prefer to remain employees at nonexecutive levels. Most self-made billionaires have high career aspirations and are founders, partners, entrepreneurs, venture capitalists, business chiefs, and risk-takers. In fact, you won't find many, if any, run-of-the-mill employees among the world's richest. You may find a few people who started as employees and advanced to executive positions. For example, Steve Ballmer of Microsoft went from employee number thirty to CEO. Those like Ballmer among the billionaires are "founding or highly dynamic employees" whose contributions attract significant company equity and wealth. When Microsoft incorporated in 1981, Ballmer owned 8 percent of the company. His decision to join a start-up and ability to gain significant equity proved extremely profitable as Microsoft grew.

Most billionaires probably didn't have riches on their minds when they started their professions. Making billions tends not to be the focus, but a byproduct, of many excellent career and business decisions. Jeff Bezos quit his well-paying job at a Wall Street firm to start Amazon because he saw tremendous growth in web usage. Jan Koum shunned employment to start WhatsApp so that he could send notifications to his friends. Perhaps Bezos and Koum dreamed of "making it" someday, but becoming billionaires wasn't their primary reason for doing what they did.

Billionaires are such because they made career choices that invited significant prosperity. Ballmer and Jeffrey Immelt (CEO of GE) shared an office at Procter & Gamble and then chose very different career paths. Ballmer took a gamble by joining a young company, which paid off, while Immelt joined an established, blue chip company. Immelt is a highly paid executive who's built a sizeable nest egg in the hundreds of millions, but he isn't a billionaire.

It isn't million-dollar salaries that make people super rich; it's company equity. As one person remarked regarding Silicon Valley and employee stock compensation, "Part of its allure is the ability for employees to get rich through ownership of the next big thing. Management competes for and incentivizes employees to drive these companies forward by making stock options and stock grants a part of their compensation package. It makes sense from the company's perspective as this portion of employee compensation does not create a draw on the company's cash balance. Instead the company simply issues stock at the appropriate time."

Established companies are limited to what they can give away in shares compared with start-ups, which use equity to secure top talent instead of high salaries. Start-ups must often bootstrap operations and keep expenses low, so executive salaries usually take a hit in exchange for company equity. This partly explains why Ballmer's net worth is far greater than Immelt's. Ballmer became uber-rich through company stock, Immelt less so through huge salaries.

FOUR-STEP PROCESS

For a person to amass riches, he or she takes these four actions:

1. Develop a good idea
2. Put the idea into action
3. Recruit individuals to join and support you
4. Grow the business

Step One: Develop a Good Idea

What is a good idea? In business, a good idea is one that can lead to advantageous and profitable outcomes. For instance, an idea that could gain first or early mover advantages and market share in a profitable sector. PayPal's founders had a good idea to become an early mover in online financial services. Today, PayPal is a leader in online payments and transactions, with over 190 million customers.

Profitability is how good ideas and companies remain afloat. On the other hand, tens of thousands of companies fold every year because they cannot generate enough profits to keep operating. For example, hundreds of unprofitable tech companies folded during the dot-com crash.

A good idea can surface in multiple ways—through a vision, market research, or desire to solve a personal problem. Steve Jobs had a robust vision to radically change the form and function of personal computing upon his return to Apple. Michael Dell focused on market research concerning cost savings by selling direct to the consumer. Jack Dorsey wanted to solve communication challenges faced by his dispatch software company, which inspired the creation of Twitter.

Individuals may develop ideas through other methods, such as brainstorming, problem-solving, improving a product or service, creating an alternative, or developing a unique offering. Furthermore, market research is useful and required at some point to validate an idea.

What an individual, or company, thinks of his or her idea isn't as important as what the marketplace and consumers think. No matter the perceived potential of an idea, consumers will ultimately determine its fate.

Do you remember a microblogging site called Jaiku? Google purchased Jaiku in 2007; it was beaten badly by Twitter and shut down in 2012. Google thought Jaiku had a "good idea," but the marketplace chose Twitter.

Blackberry was onto something with its smartphones, but its market dominance quickly eroded as consumers shifted to Apple and Android phones. Blackberry's smartphone presence is now virtually nonexistent.

Step Two: Put the Idea into Action

Does Ingvar Kamprad become a billionaire if he limits himself to just dreaming about a retail empire called Ikea? Of course not. You don't become wealthy by sitting on an idea; you must act on it. Putting an idea into action requires follow-up activities such as business planning, market research, testing, validating, securing capital, and so on.

Suppose today you came up with an idea. What would you do next? You might write your idea on paper to expand your thoughts or search online to see if your product or service already exists. You might investigate and develop your concept further. You might conduct market research, beta tests, and validation experiments. For instance, you might obtain feedback from people in your network, such as family and friends. You might consider ways of funding your idea—for example, through crowdfunding or a bank loan. You might create a suitable business structure to support your venture, such as a corporation, and you might file a patent, if applicable. Also, you might quit your full-time or part-time job to focus on your idea full-time.

Step Three: Recruit Individuals to Join and Support You

Michael Bloomberg was critical to the success of Bloomberg L.P., but he didn't grow the company by himself. Assuming your business venture is beyond one person's capabilities, you're going to need personnel to execute other functions such as legal, human resources, manufacturing, website development, and so forth.

Since your company will be a start-up, the first one hundred or so individuals to join your company (founding employees) will be integral to its success. The ability to identify top talent and contributors will come in handy.

Step Four: Grow the Business

Turning an idea into a successful venture can be financially rewarding, but it is by no means easy. Most businesses operate in competitive markets, so the task of growing comes with challenges. For example, Amazon continues to upend the United States retail sector with competitors like Sears falling by the wayside and many others declaring bankruptcy. Nevertheless, many executive and management teams succeed in growing profitable businesses.

Since entrepreneurs often take on more financial risks than employees, it's only fair that they gain more if things work out. Also, entrepreneurs understand that their individual fortunes are highly correlated to the success of their businesses. Business success equates to building a sustainable business while increasing revenues and profits annually.

Two More Considerations

There are two other steps we need to consider regarding career aspirations: individuals must keep building, and they must stay the course.

Self-made billionaires have high tendencies to **keep building** until their visions materialize.

- Jack Ma's first attempt at online domination with China Pages was a failure. Instead of quitting entrepreneurship, he launched Alibaba four years later. Ma kept building toward his vision, which led to financial success.

- Contrary to popular belief, Elon Musk didn't become a billionaire after eBay acquired PayPal. He kept building and reinvested his large windfall of $160 million into new ventures such as Tesla and SpaceX.
- Gabe Newell became one of many "Microsoft millionaires" as a developer of Windows. He eventually left Microsoft to start Valve, a video game development and digital distribution company. Valve propelled him to billionaire status.

Making hundreds of thousands or millions is enough to hamper many people's desires to keep building. For every Musk and Newell, there are thousands of millionaires who either retire early or continue working as employees.

Self-made billionaires are willing to **stay the course** longer than their nonbillionaire counterparts.

Have you heard of Ronald Wayne or Chad Hurley?

- Ronald Wayne was a co-founder of Apple with Steve Wozniak and Steve Jobs. Wayne received a 10 percent stake but relinquished his equity for $800 less than two weeks into his tenure. Had Wayne held onto his stake, he would have realized tens of billions of dollars.
- Chad Hurley cofounded YouTube in 2005, and a year later, he and his partners sold it to Alphabet (Google) for $1.65 billion. Unlike Wayne, Hurley made a fortune and is a multimillionaire set for life, but he's not a billionaire. Today, YouTube is valued at more than $70 billion. All else equal, Hurley and his partners could have been worth billions.

It's a popular theme in the start-up community to dream of being acquired and exiting quickly, but these paths do not usually create billionaires. Multiple companies offered to purchase Facebook, but

Mark Zuckerberg refused to sell. Zuckerberg could have easily made out like a bandit like Hurley, but he decided to stay the course and is now one of the richest people in the world. Furthermore, Facebook has minted multiple billionaires and wealthy investors due to its meteoric rise.

OTHER OPTIONS

Is starting a business the only way to get rich? What about investing in the stock market? <u>According</u> to financial analyst Mark Hulbert, "Investing in stocks will never make you a billionaire. The returns are just too small; the real path to wealth is by starting and selling a company. The best way to get on the list is to focus your entrepreneurial energies on producing something that the world needs. The stock market will be there after you make your fortune."

Hulbert is correct, <u>many</u> billionaires are entrepreneurial either by founding a company or joining a start-up early. Similarly, Thomas Stanley, author of *The Millionaire Next Door,* reported the following about American millionaires, "About two-thirds of us who are working are self-employed... Also, three out of four of us who are self-employed consider ourselves to be entrepreneurs." (*The Millionaire Next Door*, p. 8.) Entrepreneurship tends to be the path with the pot of gold at the end of it. On the other hand, working as an everyday employee and investing in the stock market are less likely to yield large fortunes.

Billionaires from the financial sector are usually portfolio or hedge fund managers who charge hefty performance fees and who take large positions themselves. For example, George Soros and Ray Dalio are in that category. Rarer is someone like David Cheriton who, while a professor at Stanford, became a billionaire through an early investment in Alphabet.

VALUATION

Your business is on its way and it will take at least a billion-dollar valuation (likely billions due to ownership dilution) either through earnings multiples or funding rounds to achieve a billion-dollar net worth. Secondly, even if you're achieving astronomical quarter-over-quarter revenue growth, it may not be enough for you to become a billionaire. Competition (Uber versus Didi Chuxing), new technology (mobile versus smartphones), and ever-changing regulations (Airbnb versus New York City) can easily derail your prospects. Lastly, not every business can scale or has an owner who wants to scale to billion-dollar valuations. For example, a restaurant owner who prefers to limit expansion to five locations as opposed to expanding nationwide or globally like McDonald's.

Patrick and John Collison founded Stripe, a privately held digital payments company. Both brothers are billionaires, with Stripe valued at about $9 billion. (Each brother owns roughly 11 percent of the company). How is Stripe's valuation calculated? "The company's valuation is a reflection on its size, scale, potential profitability and an unbounded market size," says Hemant Taneja, managing director at General Catalyst. Additionally, Stripe has raised $440 million in funding from various investors, including CapitalG, the late-stage investment arm of Alphabet (the relatively new name for the parent company of Google). Another opinion reads, "Stripe's valuation is partly built on the belief that more commerce will move from shop registers to websites and mobile apps, even when people are in stores, because of the advent of mobile wallets such as Apple Inc.'s Apple Pay or J.P. Morgan's Chase Pay that can be tapped or scanned at the checkout counter."

As a privately held start-up, Stripe is not required to disclose its financials publicly. Private investors and insiders have access to this information, which they use to make investment decisions. Start-up valuations tend to be based on short-term financials, internal and external projections, and funding rounds.

When a company goes public, different valuation metrics are used. Also, everyday people can freely access financials such as balance sheets, income statements, and cash flow statements. Investors use these statements and reports to make investment decisions.

Jack Ma made it easier to assess his net worth when the company he cofounded, Alibaba, went public on the New York Stock Exchange in 2014. Suppose Alibaba is trading at $100 a share and has 2.5 billion shares outstanding, Alibaba would have a value, or market capitalization, of $250 billion (share price times outstanding shares). Given Ma's 7.8 percent stake in Alibaba, while excluding his other investments, we could calculate his net worth at roughly $19.5 billion.

BILLIONAIRE INDUSTRIES (*Forbes*)

Over the past thirty years, the technology sector has been a hotbed for creating billionaires. Nine of the top thirty self-made billionaires belong to this sector. Conversely, when you consider all billionaires, other sectors outshine the tech sector.

The industry producing the most billionaires is finance and investments, with 15 percent of billionaires belonging to it. The fashion and retail category ranks second, at 12 percent, and real estate ranks third, at 9 percent.

Industry rankings fluctuate from region to region. For example, in Europe, the top industry for creating billionaires is fashion and retail, whereas in the Asia Pacific, it's real estate. Also, a country's development status influences industries. For instance, whether a country is developed, emerging, or underdeveloped typically influences its degree of technological development. In a developed country such as Canada, a robust technology sector is present compared with an underdeveloped country such as the South Pacific island nation of Vanuatu, which lacks sufficient technological infrastructure.

Industries that produce the most billionaires (as of 2016:

1. Finance and investments: 267 billionaires (15 percent of the worldwide total)
2. Fashion and retail: 221 billionaires (12 percent)
3. Real estate: 163 billionaires (9 percent)
4. Technology: 159 billionaires (9 percent)
5. Manufacturing: 157 billionaires (9 percent)

5 | PERSONALITY TRAITS: WHAT IT BOILS DOWN TO

Identifying the personality traits required to build wealth calls for a logical process. For instance, it's highly unlikely that someone who is lazy can create a billion-dollar empire since doing so requires an industrious manner. According to UBS, the three personality traits of successful billionaire entrepreneurs are smart risk-taking, obsessive business focus, and dogged determination. Successful self-made business people, millionaires, and billionaires possess these and other qualities, including these "big five" traits: openness to experience, conscientiousness, extraversion, agreeableness, and emotional stability. Personality traits must be coupled with key skills to achieve. For example, critical thinking, time management, and communication are essential skills that will never go out of style.

Of the major wealth building factors, personality is the factor that individuals have the most control over alongside career aspirations. It may not be easy to leave your country and relocate. Gender and physical modifications can be extremely costly. But the personality and attitude an individual chooses to embrace is entirely up to him or her. For example, a person can increase her curiosity by increasing her desire to know more. Here are the personality traits that well-off individuals possess.

- Entrepreneurial
- Risk-taking
- Ambitious

- High achieving
- Highly engaged
- Interpersonal
- Highly committed
- Confident
- Decisive
- Curious
- Competitive
- Unsparing
- Well-informed
- Visionary
- Charitable

Hundreds of articles discuss billionaire traits and what it takes to become one. Many of these same articles are brief and propose generic ideas that can be attached to any successful person, regardless of rank or industry. However, personality traits and the degree to which they're required are highly dependent on industry and position. For instance, do all billionaires possess good leadership skills? No, of course not. A hedge fund manager can be a below-average leader but an excellent stock picker who consistently outperforms the market. Moreover, the hedge fund manager would need to be risk-taking and highly engaged to produce above-average results. Must billionaires be innovative? No. Lei Jun, founder of Xiaomi Inc., and his partners weren't particularly innovative when they decided to enter the smartphone market after Apple, Samsung, and BlackBerry, but they were visionary. Also, many billionaires accumulate wealth from real estate holdings, which hardly invites innovation.

The qualities of self-made billionaires aren't entirely dissimilar from those of self-made millionaires except that billionaires' career paths and enterprises differ in scope and scale. For example, Ray Dalio founded Bridgewater Associates and built it into one of the world's largest hedge funds. In contrast, a hypothetical "Joe Smith" might be a successful investment adviser who makes millions, but as a small business owner, he's less likely to earn billions. That said, Dalio and Smith would probably possess similar characteristics, such as being ambitious and well-informed.

It's important not to isolate billionaires from other extremely wealthy and successful individuals. Does a self-made millionaire with a net worth of $800 million have fewer or weaker qualities than a billionaire in the same industry? Perhaps or perhaps not. We should learn about these two people before casting judgment, since only hundreds of millions separate them.

Entrepreneurial and Risk-Taking

Self-made billionaires are entrepreneurial, and they're willing to take calculated risks to achieve their goals. Billionaires at some point refuse to accept the status quo and comforts of employment in exchange for empire-building ventures. They're not the types of individuals who are satisfied with being employees under someone else's command. According to journalist Helen Coster, "It takes serious guts to abandon the comforts of an office, a two-week paycheck and a decent health care package to start a small business, let alone build an empire."

Entrepreneurship and taking chances doesn't suit everyone. Some individuals are risk-averse and prefer the sense of security associated with being an employee. However, many entrepreneurs understand that "job security" is a myth given increasing globalization, economic volatility, outsourcing, and offshoring. The idea that anyone's job is safe is a ridiculous notion, as evidenced by news of large layoffs making daily business headlines. You'll find very few lifetime employees, if any, who make the billionaire ranks unless they were founding employees in a start-up, were aggressive investors, or inherited their fortunes.

A common thread among successful entrepreneurs is their inclination to diversify their lines of business, which calls for risk-taking. Many entrepreneurs desire to keep expanding and venturing into new markets. For example, Larry Page is spearheading Alphabet into the self-driving car market, which is entirely different from the company's origins in online search and paid advertising.

Michael Bloomberg found himself unemployed after Salomon Brothers was acquired in the early 1980s. With a generous severance package, he started a company instead of seeking employment elsewhere. His company, Bloomberg L.P., has made him extremely wealthy. Bloomberg's risk-taking didn't stop in the private sector. He stepped down as CEO to assume mayoral duties of New York City in 2001. He was reelected twice and served a total of three terms. (Bloomberg served the three four-year terms after successfully petitioning for an extension of the city's term limits to three terms from two.)

Andy Beal began entrepreneurship early. At nineteen, he bought his first property, a house in Lansing, for $6,500 and then rented it out for $199 a month. Beal saw more promise in his business career and decided to drop out of Baylor University. Dropping out can be risky since studies show dropouts attract lower incomes than graduates over the long haul. Beal also took risks by buying buildings in disrepair with a goal of repairing them and selling them for profits.

Azim Premji took a gamble by dropping out of Stanford to head his family's vegetable oil and soap business in India. He grew the business and product offerings and eventually turned the company into a leading IT services corporation.

Ambitious and High Achieving

What are the chances an unambitious person or an ambitious low achiever will become a billionaire? Probably not very high. Lack of ambition explains itself in the billionaire equation, and ambition accompanied by substandard results won't take a person very far. Also, poor results move in the opposite direction of wealth accumulation.

Billionaires are ambitious, high achievers. It's these two qualities combined that produce desirable financial outcomes. Level and frequency of achievement is what separates affluent individuals from everyone else.

Cyrus Poonawalla wanted to diversify from his family stud farm in India. His drive and propensity to achieve led to building one of Asia's largest vaccine makers.

Hasso Plattner aspired to become more than an employee. He and four colleagues quit IBM to start the German software company SAP, which has become one of the largest software and programming companies globally.

Highly Engaged

Billionaires are passionate, or at least highly engaged, in their business affairs. They tackle workloads, and risks, that are often far more demanding than their employees, so they deserve the wealth they attract. They work with a high sense of urgency, and their personal and professional lives remain intertwined before and after regular working hours. Indeed, it's hard to imagine someone who is dispassionate, disengaged, or punch-clock-focused accumulating riches.

Passions can fade over time, which is why founders and entrepreneurs need to maintain extraordinary work ethics dedicated to advancing their companies. When passion and engagement fade, their companies' survival prospects diminish as well.

Mark Cuban routinely stayed up until 2:00 a.m. reading about new software and went seven years without a vacation. Jeff Bezos wasn't that much different. Early days at Amazon were characterized by working twelve-hour days, seven days a week, and being up until 3:00 a.m. to get books shipped. Michael Jordan played in as many games as he could and spent just as much time working on his skills during the offseason, courtesy of the "love of the game" clause in his contract. Warren Buffett would research stocks from sun up to sun down.

Interpersonal

No man or woman is an island. To achieve billionaire standing requires relationships, partnerships, and human capital. Relationship activities consist of communicating, leading, managing, delegating, influencing, negotiating, and motivating people toward common goals. Thus, relationship intelligence is critical to develop and possess. Entrepreneurs and business people who become wealthy do so because they have robust relationship management and interpersonal skills. Also, billionaires surround themselves with high-frequency, high achievers, and they typically allocate most of their time to a core group of individuals to further their goals.

Large employers such as Wal-Mart and McDonald's couldn't function well without solid internal and external relationship activities such as managing employees (internal) and communicating with the press (external). When employees respect and follow management, management has an easier time fulfilling company objectives. According to Boris Groysberg, professor of business administration at Harvard, "chief executives need leadership, team- and relationship building, communication and presentation, and change-management skills to thrive. These skills fall in the social and interpersonal skills bucket."

Amazon may have begun with one person's vision, but today it's a company with thousands of employees, partners, and customers. Jeff Bezos has been effective at developing and maintaining internal and external relationships despite challenges throughout the years. For instance, there was a standoff between Amazon and book publishers over pricing, which was eventually resolved. When Amazon's company culture was referred to as a "bruising workplace" where many employees can been seen crying at their desks, Bezos encouraged employees, or "Amazonians," to contact HR or him personally.

In contrast, Jack Dorsey's relationship skills have let him down at Twitter.

Dorsey, one of four Twitter co-founders, had left but returned when then-CEO Dick Costolo resigned. The other three co-founders left, but two have since returned. Twitter has experienced a high churn rate among key stakeholders, executives, and employees. The company is currently stuck in a rut and not even close to making money. Without a fully committed CEO—Dorsey also leads Square Inc.—who possesses robust relationship management skills, Twitter continues to face major obstacles. Merger and acquisition speculation for Twitter surfaced in the third quarter of 2016, but no bidders stepped up. Perhaps no one wanted to acquire and absorb Twitter's relationship challenges.

Highly Committed

If you're OK with finishing, or tend to finish, in second place or worse, billionaire status is likely to evade you. Building an empire is an arduous journey that is not for the faint of heart. It's that much more challenging for individuals born with unfavorable odds. Successful entrepreneurs are steadfast in their pursuit of world domination. They aren't focused on when they can take their next vacations but on delivering at all hours of the day. According to one study, 50 percent of self-made millionaires woke up at least three hours before their work day began.

Being ambitious and high achieving differs from being highly committed. High commitment means pushing work boundaries and exerting more effort than your colleagues. To become a billionaire requires dedication, sacrifice, and work-life imbalance.

When Steve Jobs returned to Apple in 1996, he worked from 7:00 a.m. to 9:00 p.m. every day since he was also leading Pixar. He was likely one of the last people to leave the office daily. He worked tirelessly and suffered from kidney stones. He insisted on managing both companies by consistently showing up and pushing people to make the best products possible.

Former Starbucks CEO Howard Schultz put in thirteen-hour days and talked to overseas employees at times convenient for them. He read e-mails from his thousands of employees on Saturdays and went into the office on Sundays. There's no doubt his Starbucks brew helped to keep him on task.

Zhou Qunfei was born into poverty, and being female worked against her. Her mother passed away when she was five, and her father supported the family by making bamboo baskets and chairs and repairing bicycles. Qunfei went from being a factory worker to an entrepreneur when she launched her watch lenses company in her early twenties. Her dedication had to be above average if she was to become one of China's richest women.

Confident

The path to prosperity does attract risk-taking, which requires healthy amounts of confidence and optimism. When an individual starts a business or takes a large gamble, what he or she is really saying is to heck with everyone else; I'm confident in my abilities and believe things will work out. Joan Kane, a Manhattan psychologist who works with high-powered executives, says, "People who are very successful have an incredible sense of optimism. They don't have the sense of limitations that most people have. There's no limit to their capacity to achieve and keep going. Age and family commitments don't deter them."

While self-confidence and optimism won't guarantee success, these traits are necessary to keep reaching and pushing oneself. Author and private wealth expert Russ Alan Prince says of millionaires, "Believing in yourself – truly believing in yourself – is just as important to your economic achievements as working mercilessly hard. In researching the wealth creating mindset and behaviors of self-made millionaires, it is evident that they have high self-efficacy. Self-efficacy is the belief that you can succeed in specific situations; that you will obtain your financial goals. Self-made millionaires are confident in their wealth creating abilities. They are capable and motivated to persevere when confronted with setbacks and arduous situations."

Many entrepreneurs are required to speak publicly about their companies and current events through shareholder meetings, conference calls, and live interviews. These activities require confidence and high self-esteem. Conversely, individuals seeking to avoid public speaking or media scrutiny aren't suited for entrepreneurship or executive positions.

George Soros is one of the most successful fund managers and investors in history. He generated an average annual return of more than 30 percent over thirty years. His poise prompted massive currency bets and speculative positions. In 1992, Soros bet against the British pound by short selling it and made over £1 billion in profit on that trade. Not all of his trades go as planned, but confidence keeps him going.

Francois Pinault displays self-assurance while expanding his empire from one sector to the next. He started a wood business that focused on buying and selling lumber and then expanded to retail with the acquisition of a French department store chain. He also purchased a mail-order catalog company and international auction house. Arguably, his biggest victory came when he gained control of Gucci and its popular brands, including Yves Saint Laurent and Balenciaga.

Decisive

Through his interviews with over five hundred millionaires—including Andrew Carnegie, Henry Ford, and Charles M. Schwab—*Think and Grow Rich* author Napoleon Hill found that they shared a single quality: decisiveness. Hill says, "Analysis of several hundred people who had accumulated fortunes well beyond the million-dollar mark disclosed the fact that every one of them had the habit of reaching decisions promptly, and of changing these decisions slowly, if, and when they were changed. People who fail to accumulate money, without exception, have the habit of reaching decisions, if at all, very slowly, and of changing these decisions quickly and often." (*Think and Grow Rich*, p. 148.)

Decisiveness speaks to the ability to make decisions quickly. While this trait is critical at every level of a company, it's much more so among senior executives. When executives are decisive, company operations can flow while reducing confusion and bottlenecks. If executives are indecisive, they can cripple and negatively impact the organization.

Decisiveness doesn't work in isolation; it must be accompanied by superb reasoning and decision-making skills to produce desired outcomes. Excellent decision-making abilities require a well-oiled cognitive process that can consistently select the best course of action among several possibilities. Each day, entrepreneurs and executives make many decisions relating to various internal and external business matters. Individuals who are decisive and cognitively sound will have a good chance at producing many positive results. In contrast, making too many poor decisions fast will betray an individual.

Billionaires are not impervious to bad reasoning, but their good decisions overshadow their bad ones. Warren Buffett has a fantastic investing track record due to his decisiveness and reasoning skills, but not all his investments have been winners. While Steve Case is a billionaire, his involvement in the AOL-Time Warner merger is considered one of the worst business decisions ever made. Buffett and Case, like any billionaire, have made their fair share of mistakes, but most of their decisions have been profitable, which is what produces wealth.

Curious

How did Microsoft go from personal computing to competing in the video game market? How did Wal-Mart go from a nongrocery presence to dominating supermarket sales in the United States? How did Alphabet go from being a search engine to a mighty tech conglomerate with smartphone apps and YouTube in its portfolio?

Knowing that only the strong survive and sluggishness is a one-way ticket to extinction, successful entrepreneurs embrace curiosity and competitiveness. They apply these traits to expand into different markets, lines of business, and multiple streams of income to compete for market share.

Bill Gates led Microsoft into the video game industry to compete with Sony's PlayStation, which was luring game developers away from Microsoft's Windows platform. Instead of playing possum, Microsoft launched the Xbox game console.

Sam Walton envisioned Wal-Mart as a one-stop shop to serve all its customers' needs. To achieve this, in 1988 the company launched its first Wal-Mart Supercenter, which combined discounted merchandise with groceries.

Eric Schmidt led the early expansion of Alphabet into countless forays beyond search and pay-per-click advertising. Today, Alphabet is involved in home devices, life sciences, urban innovation, drugs, and countless other initiatives.

In the immortal words of Steve Jobs, "Stay hungry. Stay foolish." Billionaires don't become self-satisfied and keep pushing boundaries no matter how ridiculous they seem. Gates, Walton, and Schmidt adopted a curious, competitive, and open-minded business approach that led their companies to new frontiers.

Unsparing

You can't make an omelet without breaking an egg, and you can't make several billions without stepping on a few toes or testing

71

regulations. One would be naive to think the path to riches is a hunky-dory love fest between rival companies and their chiefs.

Billionaires have varying degrees of ruthlessness, and they aren't necessarily the most righteous individuals concerning business operations and ethics. Some billionaires play by the rules, while others have been party to controversial activities. Mark Zuckerberg hacked into protected areas of Harvard's computer network and was accused of misleading others during the creation of Facebook. Phil Knight, directly or indirectly, exploited overseas workers through sweatshops to manufacture Nike products. Rupert Murdoch's *News of the World* newspaper (now defunct) was embroiled in phone hacking and cover-ups.

As the Internet began to flourish, a heated contest began for web browser dominance, also known as "browser wars." Netscape's Navigator had a commanding lead until Microsoft bundled its Internet Explorer (IE) browser with its Windows operating system (OS). The US government viewed Microsoft's sales strategy as anticompetitive given its OS monopoly. An antitrust case and settlement followed, leaving a blemish on Microsoft's history.

Bill Gates was the CEO of Microsoft when the decision was made to package IE with Windows. His strategy to leverage Windows was partly to blame for Navigator's dramatic decline and eventual disappearance. Gates was known to be very shrewd, competitive, and scheming. As reported, "when they hired Steve Ballmer in 1980 to run the business side of Microsoft, (co-founder Paul) Allen agreed to give him up to 5% of the company's equity. Gates went behind his back and offered Ballmer 8.75%. Allen challenged Gates on it, and Gates offered to make up the difference out of his own share." It appears Gates didn't become the richest person in the world by always playing fair or being transparent. Gates was willing to push the envelope—extend the limits of what was possible.

Well-Informed

A popular topic concerning billionaires centers on postsecondary education and the schools they did or didn't attend. Top schools such as the University of Pennsylvania, Harvard, Yale, and Stanford have an impressive stable of billionaire alumni. In contrast, 30 percent of billionaires do not have bachelor degrees. Famous nongraduates include Bill Gates, Amancio Ortega, Mark Zuckerberg, Larry Ellison, Michael Dell, Steve Jobs, Ralph Lauren, Richard Branson, Oprah Winfrey, Michele Ferrero, Li-Ka Shing, and Ingvar Kamprad.

Learning falls into various categories and types. For example, formal, informal, nonformal, auditory, visual, and so on. Successful business people draw from these buckets, but in different portions, depending on their preferences and needs. Furthermore, formal education alone isn't a recipe for prosperity. While formal learning can be beneficial to a billionaire's journey, being able to learn on the job and self-teaching are aspects that are just as important. Lastly, successful entrepreneurs remain well-informed and up-to-date, and they become subject-matter experts about their industries. Gates and Buffett often state how much they value lifelong learning and reading.

Visionary

Not every billionaire is a visionary per se, but many share this quality. Visionaries see the future of markets long before everyone else. Their minds are in continuous motion to produce new ideas and solve problems. Consequently, their creativity and innovation often create first-mover advantages (FMA)—the advantages gained by entering a market segment first.

Richard Branson has been a visionary from day one. He started a mail-order record business in his early twenties, and that led to a chain of record stores. His vision for success has evolved into the Virgin Group, which has branched out to products and services in multiple sectors—Virgin Money, Virgin Mobile, Virgin Holidays, and V Festival.

Elon Musk is a transportation visionary. He's launched SpaceX, a rocket company, and Tesla, an all-electric, zero-emissions sports car manufacturer. His mental prowess is impressive, having branched out to products for land and outer space. Musk has always been enterprising, original, and forward-thinking regarding his business endeavors. Instead of duplicating what's already available, he takes a pioneering approach to capturing new markets.

Charitable

It's easy to target the ultrawealthy as representatives of greed and inequality, but giving back through philanthropy is a high priority for them. More than 56 percent of total billionaires either undertake or are interested in pursuing philanthropic activities. They routinely give away millions, with donations exceeding $100 million becoming commonplace. The Giving Pledge has attracted over 150 billionaires who intend to donate their riches to various causes after they die. Billionaires such as duty-free shopping pioneer Charles Feeney and Bill Gates are on quests to give all, or nearly all, their money away. Lastly, billionaires are known to donate vast amounts of money to universities and cultural institutions in exchange for naming rights. For example, in 2008, David Booth and his wife donated $300 million to the University of Chicago, which renamed its business school the University of Chicago Booth School of Business. These legacy donations tend to benefit multiple parties, including indirect recipients such as students.

Billionaires can be both taking and giving. It's the balance of these two qualities that favors successful entrepreneurs. If a person is just giving of his time, for example, he won't get his work done. Conversely, if an individual just takes, he'll put his relationships in jeopardy. Billionaires appreciate the interplay between these two behaviors and manage them carefully to fulfill their objectives.

6 | TIMING: BIRTH YEAR CAN MAKE A DIFFERENCE

Birth year and timing are interesting factors when considering how some billionaires make their fortunes. Birth year is less important in countries that rank well in economic freedom and ease of doing business. In these countries, individuals can easily start businesses, so wealth accumulation need not be dependent on timing and major economic or industry events. In contrast, birth year matters more in nations that rank poorly in economic freedom and ease of conducting business. In these countries, people face business climates that are inefficient and unfriendly, so being born at the right time can prove favorable to take advantage of future economic shifts or industry revolutions. Also, being the right age and in the right place with the right connections can be advantageous.

Malcolm Gladwell, in his book *Outliers: The Story of Success*, highlights the relationship between birth years and riches. For instance, John D. Rockefeller, Andrew Carnegie, J. P. Morgan, and several other affluent Americans were born within nine years of one another, between 1831 and 1840. These individuals were of the right age to take advantage of the industrial revolution that began in the 1870s. Gladwell says, "This was when the railroads were being built and when Wall Street emerged. It was when industrial manufacturing started in earnest. It was when all the rules by which the traditional economy had functioned were broken and remade. What this list says is that it really matters how old you were when that transformation happened. If you were born in the late 1840s, you missed it. You were too young to take advantage of that moment. If you were born in the 1820s you were too old: your mindset was shaped by the pre–Civil War paradigm. But there was a particular, narrow nine-year window that was just perfect for seeing the potential that the future held."

Gladwell expands his birth year theory to Silicon Valley billionaires such as Bill Gates, Steve Jobs, Steve Ballmer, and others. He suggests that tech billionaires who were born during the mid-1950s were of the right age by the time the personal computer era began by 1975. He says, "If you were more than a few years out of college in 1975, then you belonged to the old paradigm. You had just bought a house. You're married. A baby is on the way. You're in no position to give up a good job and pension for some pie-in-the-sky $397 computer kit. So let's rule out all those born before, say, 1952. At the same time, though, you don't want to be too young. You really want to get in on the ground floor, right in 1975, and you can't do that if you're still in high school. So let's also rule out anyone born after, say, 1958. The perfect age to be in 1975, in other words, is old enough to be a part of the coming revolution but not so old that you missed it. Ideally, you want to be twenty or twenty-one, which is to say, born in 1954 or 1955." When were Bill Gates and other tech billionaires born?

- Bill Gates: October 28, 1955
- Paul Allen: January 21, 1953
- Steve Ballmer: March 24, 1956
- Steve Jobs: February 24, 1955
- Eric Schmidt: April 27, 1955
- Bill Joy: November 8, 1954
- Scott McNealy: November 13, 1954

To Gladwell's credit, birth years and timing can explain why a certain group of individuals were favored to amass fortunes.

However, his theory doesn't apply across the board. Michael Dell (Dell Inc.) was born in 1965, ten years after what Gladwell calls the "perfect birth date." Larry Ellison (Oracle Corp.) was born on August 17, 1944, and Gordon Moore (Intel Corp.) on January 3, 1929. These individuals made their fortunes in computing and software despite not being born between 1952 and 1958.

Nobody should count on a birth year as a ticket to riches. Financial success relies on being able to take advantage of industry and economic shifts given that the person has the right career goals and personal traits. (Gender and race also influence prospects.) People who were born around 1955 without the same programming abilities as Gates and Joy wouldn't have been equipped to capitalize on the personal computer boom. Gates and his peers were extremely fortunate to get a leg up on everyone else through what Gladwell refers to as "The 10,000-Hour Rule." The principle holds that ten thousand hours of "deliberate practice" are needed to become world-class in any field. When the PC market was about to explode, Gates and others had possessed the necessary hours and know-how.

In places such as the United States, Hong Kong, and Australia, probusiness climates allow entrepreneurs to start businesses easily, which mutes the relevance of birth year and timing. Individuals like Michael Dell can enter markets as they wish with few barriers to entry (except for possibly capital requirements). On the other hand, birth year becomes more relevant in countries where economic opportunities and mobility are suppressed, such as Russia.

Before the fall of the Soviet Union, communism and a command economy yielded low levels of economic freedom, ease of doing business, and entrepreneurial opportunities. When the Soviet Union fell in the early 1990s, it ushered in the first stages of capitalism. Russian privatization of state assets allowed for select individuals to own companies and achieve financial prosperity. This major economic shift produced the first generation of Russian billionaires, or oligarchs. When were these Russian oligarchs born?

- Boris Berezovsky: January 23, 1946
- Vitaly Malkin: September 16, 1952
- Vladimir Gusinsky: October 6, 1952
- Alexander Smolensky: July 6, 1954
- Pyotr Aven: March 16, 1955
- Vladimir Vinogradov: September 19, 1955
- Vladimir Potanin: January 3, 1961
- Mikhail Khodorkovsky: June 26, 1963
- Mikhail Fridman: April 21, 1964

For the most part, it was advantageous to be a Russian male born in the 1950s and early '60s. During Russia's transformation, these individuals were in their twenties and thirties and ripe to lead businesses. They were not too young or too old to capitalize on market liberalization opportunities. Still, it's worth noting that Russian oligarch status is much more complex than birth year alone.

Political corruption, cronyism, and backroom deals engulfed the privatization process and ownership assignments. Some Russian oligarchs have since been jailed and stripped of their fortunes while others have been the subject of murder conspiracies. You could say it's scary being a Russian billionaire given Russia's intense political and business environment. Russia, under Putin, arguably has changed, but capitalism has yet to reach Western standards. Russia has made strides, but it still ranks terribly in economic freedom and wealth equality compared with other free market societies. Putin's reign means Russians must still rely on factors such as birth year, gender, and connections to become super rich as major economic events unfold. Unfortunately, career aspirations and personality traits have less relevance in Russia.

Another area of discussion regarding birth year and wealth centers around age—at what age do most individuals reach billionaire status? While the average billionaire is in his or her sixties, the age at which a person becomes wealthy depends mostly on his or her unique journey. Here's a <u>list</u> of several well-known billionaires and the ages when they reached the milestone.

- Mark Zuckerberg: 23
- Evan Spiegel: 25
- Larry Page: 30
- Bill Gates: 31
- Jeff Bezos: 35
- Mark Cuban: 40
- Richard Branson: 41
- Elon Musk: 41
- Meg Whitman: 42
- Zhou Qunfei: 45
- Larry Ellison: 49
- Oprah Winfrey: 49
- Carlos Slim: 51
- George Lucas: 52
- Warren Buffett: 56

7 | X FACTOR: WHAT'S UNIQUE TO EACH BILLIONAIRE

By now, it should be clearer as to which factors influence billionaire treasures. However, the factors discussed until now don't do enough to separate affluent individuals from nonaffluent ones. Tens of thousands of people are born in free market countries to successful parents, yet they don't become ultrawealthy. There is one more facet that is unique to each billionaire and separates that person from everyone else.

An X factor is a unique circumstance, event, quality, or person that has had a strong but unpredictable influence on an individual. X factors can be life-changing events that propel individuals to greater heights and riches. For example, opportunities that stem from attending a prestigious private or Ivy League school or a major shift in economic policy. Depending on the billionaire, he or she may have experienced one or multiple X factors. Examples of X factors include:

- Born to an upper-class family
- Relationship to a key person or people—parent, friend, colleague, and so on
- Relationship with a mentor or coach
- Death of a parent
- Significant childhood adversity
- School attended
- Emigration
- Impact from a major political, economic or industry event

From the outside looking in, we are limited to analyzing public information about billionaires. While billionaires may point to X factors that dramatically shaped their successes, the public might assume something completely different. Secondly, billionaires may not be fully aware of their paths to riches. Even if people are very introspective and self-aware, it doesn't mean they can be all-knowing regarding the events that shaped their lives. Given the limitations of public information, we'll speculate at a high level about the critical events, people, and qualities that shaped the following billionaires.

Bill Gates—United States

Gates couldn't have wished for a better start in life. He was raised in an upper-class family, and his father was a prominent lawyer in Seattle, Washington. All the key factors aligned in his favor, and through private school education, he gained exposure to computer programming long before the masses could buy personal computers. Gates embraced entrepreneurship and had the personality traits to lead Microsoft to success. Gates is said to have been born at the "perfect time" to capitalize on the growth of personal computing in the 1980s and '90s.

Factor	In Favor	Against
Residing country	☐	
Gender	☐	
Race	☐	
Career aspirations	☐	
Personality traits	☐	
Birth year	☐	
X factors	• Leveraged a privileged start • Exposed to computing and programming before the PC market explosion • Created a virtual monopoly with the Windows operating system • Relationships with Paul Allen and Steve Ballmer were critical to the growth of Microsoft	

Amancio Ortega—Spain

Ortega is truly an anomaly because he ranks so high on billionaire lists but has humble beginnings. Instead of the upper-class treatment most eventual billionaires receive at birth, Ortega was born into a family that eked out a meager existence. His father was a railroad worker, and his mother was a housemaid. He dropped out of school and began working at the age of thirteen, which helped to cultivate his entrepreneurial prowess and shrewdness. Through retail and fashion innovation and savvy, Ortega has built Zara into a global brand and the world's largest clothing retailer.

Factor	In Favor	Against
Residing country	☐	
Gender	☐	
Race	☐	
Career aspirations	☐	
Personality traits	☐	
Birth year	N/A	
X factors	• Relocated to another town, where he learned to make clothes by hand • Developed an above-average business IQ from starting work in his early teens • Humble and highly committed • Focused on innovation—"fast fashion"	

Warren Buffett—United States

Like Gates, Buffett had everything going for him from day one. Buffett's father was an entrepreneur and investor turned US congressman, which provided Buffett with unique opportunities and connections. He jumped on board investing quite early and bought his first stock a year after visiting the New York Stock Exchange at age eleven. Buffett honed his investment knowledge at Columbia under the tutelage of Benjamin Graham and David Dodd, prominent authorities and authors on the topic of securities analysis. Buffett worked as a securities analyst and stockbroker before starting an investment firm. His investment track record and ability to beat the markets over the years has culminated in outstanding returns for investors.

Factor	In Favor	Against
Residing country	☐	
Gender	☐	
Race	☐	
Career aspirations	☐	
Personality traits	☐	
Birth year	N/A	
X factors	• Leveraged a privileged start and family connections • Learned from Benjamin Graham and David Dodd • Relationship with Charlie Munger, his lifelong business partner, was critical to the growth of Berkshire Hathaway	

Carlos Slim Helú—Mexico

Slim's father, Julián Slim Haddad, migrated to Mexico, operated a dry goods store, and then invested in commercial real estate, which made his family wealthy. The Slims' family fortune offset the unfavorable prospects of Mexico (country of residence). Slim worked at his family's company before studying civil engineering. He became a stockbroker and opened a brokerage firm. Slim invested wisely in a variety of businesses and amassed millions in his twenties. After that, he bought companies at depressed valuations, and as his holdings grew, so did his pocketbook.

Factor	In Favor	Against
Residing country		☐
Gender	☐	
Race	☐	
Career aspirations	☐	
Personality traits	☐	
Birth year	N/A	
X factors	<ul><li>Leveraged a privileged start</li><li>Raised by entrepreneurs</li><li>Started a stock brokerage in his twenties (How many Mexicans could open stock brokerages at that time?)</li><li>Developed a high investing acumen</li></ul>	

85

Jeff Bezos—United States

Bezos demonstrated an impressive academic pedigree in becoming a high school valedictorian, National Merit Scholar, and Silver Knight award winner for science. Also, he graduated from Princeton with a bachelor of science in engineering. Bezos discovered how fast the Internet was growing in the mid-1990s and acted on it by launching Amazon to gain first-mover advantages in online retail.

Factor	In Favor	Against
Residing country	☐	
Gender	☐	
Race	☐	
Career aspirations	☐	
Personality traits	☐	
Birth year	☐	
X factors	• Interested in science as a teenager • High academic achiever • Quit job to pursue entrepreneurship • Timeliness and courage to start Amazon	

Bernard Arnault—France

After graduation, Arnault joined his father's company and convinced him to pivot the business from construction to real estate. After succeeding his father and becoming CEO, Arnault pivoted again to luxury goods and aggressively acquired popular brands such as Christian Dior, LVMH, Marc Jacobs, and Sephora.

Factor	In Favor	Against
Residing country	☐	
Gender	☐	
Race	☐	
Career aspirations	☐	
Personality traits	☐	
Birth year	N/A	
X factors	<ul><li>Leveraged a privileged start</li><li>Raised by entrepreneurs</li><li>Took over the family business</li><li>Excellent deal-making and negotiating abilities</li></ul>	

George Soros—United States

Soros escaped Nazi-occupied Hungary and moved around quite a bit before settling in America. He graduated from the London School of Economics and Political Science and worked at a few brokerages before launching his company, Soros Fund Management. He's considered one of the greatest investors in history and is well-known for taking billion-dollar speculative positions in foreign currencies. Soros has given billions away to charitable causes and is very active in US and global politics.

Factor	In Favor	Against
Residing country	☐	
Gender	☐	
Race	☐	
Career aspirations	☐	
Personality traits	☐	
Birth year	N/A	
X factors	• Emigrated to England to escape Nazi rule • Studied at the London School of Economics • Relocated to New York City to enter finance • Relationship with Jim Rogers, co-founder of the Quantum Fund, was vital to business growth • Huge appetite for risk-taking	

Aliko Dangote—Nigeria

Dangote was born to a prominent business family, which offset the disadvantages of living in Nigeria. He entered entrepreneurship early with a commodity and building supplies business, which he's built into a manufacturing conglomerate. In America, Canada, and other Western countries, the odds would have been against Dangote to succeed due to his race. However, his race was a non-issue living in black-majority Nigeria.

Factor	In Favor	Against
Residing country		☐
Gender	☐	
Race	☐	
Career aspirations	☐	
Personality traits	☐	
Birth year	N/A	
X factors	<ul><li>Leveraged a privileged start</li><li>Raised by entrepreneurs</li><li>Received a loan from his uncle to start his business (How many Nigerians could easily get business loans at that time?)</li><li>Established the Dangote Group at age twenty</li></ul>	

Azim Premji—India

Premji's father was a noted businessman who founded Western Indian Vegetable Products (Wipro) Ltd., a consumer goods manufacturer. After receiving news of his father's death, Premji returned home to manage the family business. He expanded Wipro before pivoting from soap to information technology. Today, India's a much more hospitable and business-friendly country, but Premji thrived when India faced significant economic challenges.

Factor	In Favor	Against
Residing country		☐
Gender	☐	
Race	☐	
Career aspirations	☐	
Personality traits	☐	
Birth year	N/A	
X factors	<ul><li>Leveraged a privileged start</li><li>Raised by entrepreneurs</li><li>Attended Stanford</li><li>Took over the family business after his father died</li></ul>	

Henry Sy—Philippines

Sy moved from China to the Philippines at age twelve, where he joined his father in Manila. He worked at his father's neighborhood store, selling rice, sardines, and soap. The Philippines, as opposed to China, was likely more fertile for Sy's business pursuits, but not ideal as a country of residence. After World War II ended, he started a business selling shoes. Years later, he opened a department store, ShoeMart, and then he opened malls nationally that sold low-priced consumer goods.

Factor	In Favor	Against
Residing country		☐
Gender	☐	
Race	☐	
Career aspirations	☐	
Personality traits	☐	
Birth year	N/A	
X factors	<ul><li>Moved to the Philippines</li><li>Raised by entrepreneurs</li><li>Entered entrepreneurship early</li><li>Keen observer and opportunist</li></ul>	

Patrick Soon-Shiong—United States

Soon-Shiong grew up in a medical family with a father who was a doctor. His parents passed their travel instincts to him when they fled China during the World War II Japanese occupation. After receiving his medical degree in Johannesburg, Soon-Shiong moved to the United States to start surgical training at the University of California. Instead of choosing conventional career paths, Soon-Shiong took a leap of faith and founded a biotechnology company.

Factor	In Favor	Against
Residing country	☐	
Gender	☐	
Race		☐
Career aspirations	☐	
Personality traits	☐	
Birth year	N/A	
X factors	<ul><li>Leveraged a privileged start</li><li>Father worked as a village doctor</li><li>Moved to the United States from South Africa to start surgical training at UCLA</li><li>Entered entrepreneurship instead of remaining in academia or in medicine working as a physician</li></ul>	

Masayoshi Son—Japan

Son's parents did him a huge favor by adopting a Japanese surname to blend in and assimilate. Had Son stuck out as a Korean, the odds of experiencing discrimination and setbacks would have been much higher. A chance meeting with Den Fujita, founder of McDonald's Japan, inspired Son to travel to the United States to study. He studied computer science and economics, which prepared him to enter the IT industry upon returning to Japan. He decision to return to Japan—instead of remaining in the United States—made race a non-issue.

Factor	In Favor	Against
Residing country	☐	
Gender	☐	
Race	☐	
Career aspirations	☐	
Personality traits	☐	
Birth year	☐	
X factors	• Parents adopted a Japanese surname • Den Fujita advised Son to study in the United States • Studied at UCLA • Returned to Japan to enter entrepreneurship	

Zhang Xin—China

Xin grew up in poverty and began working as a factory laborer at age fourteen. By the age of twenty, she used her savings to fly to Britain, where she studied at the universities of Sussex and Cambridge. Alongside many other successful Goldman Sachs alumni, Xin parlayed her work experience into real estate endeavors. Although gender was not on Xin's side, returning to China benefited her from a racial standpoint. Had she remained in Britain or America, gender and race would have been roadblocks.

Factor	In Favor	Against
Residing country	☐	
Gender		☐
Race	☐	
Career aspirations	☐	
Personality traits	☐	
Birth year	N/A	
X factors	<ul><li>Strong work ethic and determination</li><li>Above-average business IQ forged from starting work at age fourteen</li><li>Studied in Britain and worked in America at Goldman Sachs</li><li>Returned to Hong Kong to enter entrepreneurship</li></ul>	

Oprah Winfrey—United States

Winfrey is a poster child for rags-to-riches stories. Born into poverty, black, female, and sexually abused, the odds of her becoming a millionaire, never mind a billionaire, were against her. To overcome her rough start, she reached for the stars with high career aspirations. After completing university, she hosted a TV chat show in her early twenties. Winfrey's brilliant personality yielded career advancement in TV and film. She launched *The Oprah Winfrey Show* in 1986 as a nationally syndicated program and currently heads the Oprah Winfrey Network (OWN).

Factor	In Favor	Against
Residing country	☐	
Gender		☐
Race		☐
Career aspirations	☐	
Personality traits	☐	
Birth year	N/A	
X factors	• High career aspirations • Exceptional personality traits • Multitalented entertainer • Excellent relationship and interpersonal skills	

8 | Once a Billionaire, Not Always a Billionaire

One might assume that making the billionaire ranks guarantees permanent residency in those ranks, but that is hardly the case. Only 44 percent of billionaires from 1995 are still around as billionaires. So, what happened to the 56 percent who are no longer billionaires? Death, business failure, economic events, dilution of wealth, family misfortunes, and taxes are just some of the culprits.

1. Business Failure and Economic Events

Elizabeth Holmes at one point had an estimated net worth of $4.5 billion. Her net worth was tied to her company, Theranos, a blood-extracting and testing company that she founded in 2003. Theranos had been valued at $9 billion, making Holmes a billionaire in her early thirties. However, questionable laboratory results and pressure from outsiders led to a dramatic decline in Theranos's valuation and prospects. Today, Holmes's net worth is valued at zero.

BlackBerry Ltd., formerly Research in Motion Ltd., was a frontrunner during the mass adoption of smartphones. At their peak, between 2007and 2008, BlackBerry smartphones held a significant market share until Apple iPhones and Google Android phones entered the market. As of 2016, BlackBerry stopped manufacturing smartphones in-house due to declining demand. Instead, it now offers smartphones through business partnerships. For instance, sourcing handsets from Alcatel with BlackBerry branding.

In 2007, BlackBerry's stock hit an all-time high of more than $230 a share, and *Forbes* valued the co-founders, Mike Lazaridis and

Jim Balsillie, at <u>$3 billion</u> apiece. However, their estimated fortunes came crashing down with a substantial decrease in Blackberry's share price. The co-founders dropped off *Forbes*'s list in 2012.

Holmes, Lazaridis, and Balsillie are common examples of billionaires whose business hardships caused significant decreases in wealth. The list of the world's wealthiest from *Forbes*, and other rich lists, typically report many new entrants and exits from year to year. For example, <u>221 people</u> fell off the 2016 *Forbes* list from 2015, while 198 newcomers joined the ranks.

Billionaires who have significant stakes in their businesses without ample diversification expose themselves to major fluctuations in net worth. In contrast, billionaires such as Bill Gates and Warren Buffett are less susceptible to individual business risk or systemic risk because they are well-diversified through various investments. While diversification is a recommended investment strategy, it can only do so much to protect against systemic risk—the uncertainty inherent in an entire market or market segment. For example, there were the financial downturns of the Asian Financial Crisis in 1997, the dot-com bubble collapse from 1999 to 2001, and the Great Recession of the late 2000s. During these crises, even well-diversified portfolios dropped in values.

Masayoshi Son is an example of how major economic events can impact riches. In 1981 in Japan, Son started SoftBank, a technology conglomerate. Son directed SoftBank to invest in technology start-ups as the Internet took off in the 1990s. When the dot-com bubble burst, SoftBank lost 98 percent of its value, and Son's net worth fell by more than <u>$70 billion</u>.

Son has since rebuilt SoftBank and his billionaire status. Today, SoftBank is one of the world's <u>largest public</u> companies, with billions in revenue, and Son's net worth is estimated at <u>$21 billion</u> (as of February 21, 2017).

A serial entrepreneur, Eike Batista launched multiple companies in the mining and energy industry. In 2012, Batista was the richest man in Brazil and eighth-richest in the world; his net worth was estimated at $34.5 billion. A year later, it was valued at somewhere between $100 and $400 million, which has decreased further by other accounts. A downturn in commodity and natural resource prices, alongside overly optimistic business projections and bad management, significantly crippled the value of his companies and his own net worth. Unlike Son, Batista has yet to make a comeback. For now, his promises of becoming the world's richest man must wait while he sits in prison.

In another example of how systemic risk can impact businesses and wealth, in 2015 Nigerian and Russian billionaires experienced dramatic decreases in their riches due to falling commodity prices. The fortune of Aliko Dangote, head of African's largest cement producer, dropped to $14.7 billion from $25 billion, and the number of Russian billionaires dropped to 88 in 2015 from 111 in 2014.

While unfavorable business and economic events can have adverse effects on billionaires, the opposite is true for creating billionaires. Before the dot-com crash, many founders sold their companies and became millionaires and billionaires. For example, there's American businessman Mark Cuban, who sold Broadcast.com for $5.7 billion in 1999. Also, those who survived the crash and continued to grow their businesses—for example, Amazon founder Jeff Bezos and eBay auction site founder Pierre Omidyar—remain billionaires today.

Cuban cofounded Broadcast.com in 1995. Broadcast was considered a leading destination for audio and video streaming, and it caught the attention of Yahoo, another dot-com flyer. In April 1999, Yahoo acquired Broadcast for $5.7 billion, making Cuban an instant billionaire because of his stake in the company. While the deal worked out for Cuban, Yahoo's acquisition was extremely boneheaded. Remnants of Broadcast are virtually nonexistent.

2. DILUTION OF WEALTH

Billionaires succumb to death, just like everyone else, and their fortunes spread to family, friends, charitable entities, and other beneficiaries. As more and more inheritors claim pieces of the pie, the wealth is diluted by new stakeholders.

The transfer of wealth is inevitable, and prudent billionaires work with financial and estate planners to ensure smooth transitions take place. If alive today, Sam Walton, founder of Wal-Mart Stores Inc., would be worth well over $100 billion. He passed away in 1992, and his wealth transferred to his wife and four children. Since the passing of his wife and one child, fortunes have continued to pass from one generation to the next. Currently, seven Walton family members are billionaires, from Sam's children to grandchildren. Given the size of the Walton fortune, it will be a few more generations before no Waltons are billionaires (assuming no catastrophic business or economic events occur).

The transfer of wealth isn't an event that only happens at death. Some billionaires take a proactive approach to handing over their assets as part of succession planning or to maintain family control of their businesses. For instance, Abigail Johnson inherited shares of Fidelity Investments while her father ran the company and long before she became chief executive officer. Norwegian industrialist and investor Johan Andresen transferred 42 percent ownership of the family's investment firm, Ferd, to each of his daughters before they turned twenty-one. He was in his forties when the transfer took place.

Billionaires tend to have very complex business and estate dealings that they should address while legally competent and able— not during the final stages of their lives. When affluent individuals aren't diligent about wealth and estate planning, family squabbles can ensue. Sometimes we see these quarrels unfold publicly. The Redstones are an example of how transitioning wealth to future generations can become troublesome.

Sumner Redstone (executive chair of CBS and Viacom until February 2016) has experienced feuding and lawsuits from family members and key stakeholders regarding the control of his empire. A power struggle and suggestions of manipulation by his daughter come in the wake of questions about his health and competency. Redstone, it appears, hadn't done enough to solidify his wealth and succession plans to the point where conflicts and legal drama wouldn't surface. Lawsuits and settlements are how the transfer of his riches is playing out.

Earmarking billions for charity instead of family members has become a common alternative for billionaires. The Giving Pledge is an effort to help address society's most pressing problems by inviting the world's wealthiest individuals and families to commit to giving more than half of their wealth to philanthropy or charitable causes either during their lifetime or in their wills. It specifically targets billionaires and was launched by Bill Gates and Warren Buffett in 2010. To date, over 150 pledgers have joined a global effort to help address society's biggest issues from poverty alleviation to health care to education. The pledge does not involve pooling any money or committing to any specific cause. It only asks that those who commit to the group give away most of their wealth either while they are alive or after death. One could equate the Giving Pledge and similar efforts to a redistribution of wealth to those who need it most.

Billionaires who give the bulk of their fortunes to causes will undoubtedly downgrade their families to nonbillionaire statuses. Bill Gates is fine with this and states, "It's not a favor to kids to have them have huge sums of wealth. It distorts anything they might do, creating their own path. Our kids will receive a great education and some money, so they are never going to be poorly off, but they'll go out and have their own career."

Divorce is another life event that can dramatically reduce wealth. In the United States, marital or community property divides in half between spouses who don't have a prenuptial agreement that states otherwise. In the case of a fortune that is amassed during marriage, a divorce could split the couple's assets in half. For instance, Bob and Shelia Johnson founded Black Entertainment Television (BET). Their divorce and sagging investments left them both with fortunes under a billion.

3. FAMILY MISFORTUNES

Cornelius "Commodore" Vanderbilt built one of America's great empires. His railroad and transportation conglomerate made him one of the world's richest people during the 1800s. He amassed a $100 million fortune by the time of his death. His son Billy Vanderbilt inherited a large stake and doubled the family fortune. However, it was the passing of the baton to Billy Vanderbilt's kids that began the decline of family prosperity.

Third-generation Cornelius Vanderbilt II and William Vanderbilt stopped growing the family treasure, instead choosing to focus on lavish lifestyles and philanthropic activities. Lack of interest in the business and increases in spending led to the undoing of the Vanderbilt fortune. Fourth- and fifth-generation Vanderbilts decreased the fortune through spending, financial mismanagement, and further dilution among descendants, leaving future generations with nothing. Sixth-generation Vanderbilt Anderson Cooper, a prominent news anchor, has said, "My mom has made clear to me that there's no trust fund."

The Vanderbilts are one of many riches-to-rags stories. As the old saying goes, "The first generation makes it, the second generation spends it, and the third generation blows it." "Seventy percent of wealthy families lose their wealth by the second generation, and a stunning 90 percent by the third," says The Williams Group, an intergenerational financial and estate planning firm.

The Stroh story isn't that dissimilar from that of the Vanderbilts. Bernhard Stroh founded Stroh Brewery in 1850, and by the 1980s, Stroh Brewery was a top-three American brewer, valued at $700 million. However, aggressive expansion, heavy debt, and mismanagement eventually led to the downfall and sale of Stroh to the Pabst Brewing Company in 1999. In the 1980s, seven fourth-generation Stroh family members received $400,000 a year, while other third- and fifth-generation members received differing amounts.

Checks were doled out until 2008, when the family fortune was completely exhausted.

What can we learn from the Vanderbilt and Stroh families? Prosperity through generations isn't guaranteed, irrespective of how large the fortune. Secondly, the erosion of riches is the result of a lack of planning, responsibility, communication, financial discipline, and investment savvy, coupled with not having professional guidance to assist with asset management. Had the proper financial and estate planning measures been taken, Vanderbilt and Stroh family members might still be attracting income like the Rockefellers.

John D. Rockefeller Sr. built a formidable oil monopoly in the 1800s. In 1917, he gave his only son, John Jr., $460 million (about $5 billion in today's dollars). In 1934, John Jr. established trusts for his children that consisted of company stock and real estate holdings. These trusts still hold the bulk of the fortune. Another set of trusts was set up in 1952 for his grandchildren—fourth-generation family members.

When Rockefeller family members die, their trusts divide into new trusts for future generations. This process was designed to ensure descendants could live well. Decades later, the Rockefeller family has a net worth valuation of $11 billion (as of August 2, 2017). As a nod to the importance of professional guidance, there are two hundred or so professionals who manage the Rockefeller fortune and assist with income taxes, philanthropic endeavors, and legal work.

4.   ESTATE AND INHERITANCE TAX

Inheritance tax, like inflation, is a wealth erosion factor. To prevent billions from moving freely from one generation to the next, governments levy high tax rates on inheritances. For instance, here is the percentage taken by inheritance tax for some countries: Japan, 55 percent; South Korea, 50 percent; France, 45 percent; and the United

States, 40 percent. Exemptions aside, estate and inheritance taxes greatly reduce intergenerational wealth.

HOW BILLIONAIRES INVEST

How do billionaires invest? Some billionaires—including Warren Buffett, George Soros, and John Paulson—are professional money managers, and through public filings we can learn about their funds' holdings.

Increased regulations in the United States have produced greater transparency among investment managers, who are required to file form 13F. Form 13F is a filing with the Securities and Exchange Commission (SEC). The form is also known as the Information Required of Institutional Investment Managers Form. It is a quarterly filing required of institutional investment managers with over $100 million in qualifying assets. Since hedge funds attract affluent individuals and family offices, they can shed light on where the "smart money" is flowing. On the other hand, if you're a billionaire or wealthy individual not in the finance industry, what you share with the public is mostly at your discretion unless you decide to take a large position in a publicly traded company.

When a person or group of persons acquires beneficial ownership of more than 5 percent of a voting class of a company's equity securities—registered under Section 12 of the Securities Exchange Act of 1934—that person or those persons are required to file a Schedule 13D with the SEC. Schedule 13D reports the acquisition and other information within ten days after the purchase.

Bill Gates has been very transparent about his investments through his holding company and charitable foundation. There are various reports available on the web regarding his holdings. Through Bezos Expeditions, Jeff Bezos's personal investment company, anyone can get a glimpse of his holdings. For example, he has invested in Airbnb, Business Insider, Remitly, and Uber.

It's hit or miss when trying to figure out exactly what billionaires hold, but news headlines and a bit of research can tip us off. Former Microsoft CEO Steve Ballmer is one of many billionaires who owns a sports franchise. Telecommunications leader John Malone has purchased enough land to become the largest private US landowner, with 2.2 million acres in nine states. Many billionaires have multiple real estate properties in their portfolios. Lastly, it's safe to assume that billionaires have a great deal of wealth tied up in their businesses.

POLITICAL ACTIVITY

Billionaires get involved in politics not because they necessarily need to, but because they want to influence policy, tax rates, industry regulations, public sentiment, and other critical matters. They attempt to influence government and elections by making large contributions and supporting candidates publicly. Also, some hire lobbyists who seek to persuade members of government, such as members of Congress, to enact legislation that would benefit their activities. Research has shown that the policy preferences of the very wealthy consistently prevail over the preferences of middle-class and poor voters.

Wealthy Americans are contributing millions to their parties. A 2013 study found that the top 0.01 percent of political donors, approximately twenty-four thousand people, accounted for more than 40 percent of campaign contributions, up from about 10 percent in the 1980s. As for supporting early efforts to secure the White House in 2016, just 158 families, along with the companies they owned or controlled, contributed $176 million in the first phase of the campaign cycle. The increase in legal and allowable contributions have found a pathway through a Supreme Court decision in the case of Citizens United, which gave corporate entities greater leeway to support candidates through contributions to "super political action committees" or super PACs. As for donor profiles, these individuals are overwhelmingly white, male, rich, and self-made, often hailing from finance and energy sectors.

Big money in politics has become increasingly visible globally. A few billionaires have either run for or become president, including Ross Perot (United States), Donald Trump (United States), Thaksin Shinawatra (Thailand), and Silvio Berlusconi (Italy).

More than one in seven of the 1,271 richest Chinese are serving in parliament or its advisory body. These 203 delegates are collectively worth over $460 billion. For some perspective, the richest representative in the US government would be the 166th richest member of China's government.

In what shaped up to be an interesting election year in the United States, billionaires came out of the woodwork to be heard and seen. Donald Trump won the 2016 election and fellow billionaires—including Peter Thiel, Sheldon Adelson, Woody Johnson, and Carl Icahn—supported him. For instance, Adelson and his wife, Miriam, donated millions to Republican super PACs, the third-party groups that collect unlimited funds from wealthy donors to support or oppose any candidate or issue they choose. Hillary Clinton, Trump's Democratic opponent, attracted support from Warren Buffett, Mark Cuban, Michael Bloomberg, and George Soros. Soros spent $1 million on Obama's reelection effort in 2012 and pledged $25.5 million to defeat George W. Bush in the 2004 presidential election. Additionally, he was a booster and key member of the "Ready for Hillary" super PAC, to which he donated $11.9 million for Clinton's cause.

Support for the candidates didn't stop at contributions and public appearances. Name-dropping at debates and Twitter feuds—such as Trump versus Mark Cuban—have become commonplace in politics.

9 | Is Your Wallet Half Full or Half Empty?

There was a time when I was in awe of wealthy individuals and dumbfounded as to how they achieved amazing prosperity. I realize now that accumulating wealth is dependent on various factors, and it's easy for me to understand how someone became rich. Residing in a G7 or progressive G20 county produces ample economic opportunities. Race and gender are obvious obstacles a person might have faced. Career paths and character traits are always telling. Then, I consider x factors, which often point to social class, a prestigious school attended, or a key person in that individual's life. In fact, enough data is available to predict a person's probability of becoming wealthy in the United States. For example, What Are Your Odds of Becoming a Millionaire? published by Bloomberg L.P. discusses the odds of becoming a millionaire based on race. Combine this research with other data points such as gender, location, parents' income, and so on, and we get much closer to correctly predicting individual outcomes.

Concerning net worth, you shouldn't envy or compare yourself to others because no two individuals share the same set of experiences. Does Warren Buffett become one of the richest people in the world if many events don't align in his favor? Probably not, which is why most people who don't get the breaks he did won't become billionaires. Buffett, like many millionaires and billionaires, are set up to achieve financial success from birth. The odds are stacked in their favor as they accumulate advantages before everyone else.

What's important is that you understand why you are where you are compared with others. You should focus on making intelligent professional and personal decisions to improve your circumstances. For instance, changing countries or locations to experience better opportunities. Finally, you should seriously consider how your career aspirations and personality traits are impacting your income and wealth.

Rightfully or wrongfully a lot is made of billionaires in business and news circles as if to say they are that much different from nonbillionaires. Billionaires have a lot of money, but they breathe the same air as everyone else and what should be of interest is how they use their fortunes for the greater good of humankind. For example, the Bill & Melinda Gates Foundation is worthy charitable initiative that benefit millions of people. Also, relative financial success should be appreciated just as much as absolute success. For instance, rags to riches stories should be celebrated—if not more so—than rich to richer stories, which is why I have a lot of professional respect for people like Ikea founder Ingvar Kamprad, Ursula Burns— Chairwoman and former CEO of Xerox, and John Paul DeJoria of Patrón Spirits and Paul Mitchell Systems.

If you want to achieve financial success, where do you go from here? If you are residing in a country or area with average to unfavorable economic prospects, you might consider moving. If you are a female who's hit the glass ceiling, you might seek employment at a company that practices inclusion and diversity. If you are a minority or feel as though you are getting second class treatment in a country or company, you might explore a range of options. If you are stuck in a dead-end job, you might review your career goals and consider part- or full-time entrepreneurship. If your personality doesn't favor fortunes, you might focus on self-improvement. If your skills don't command a high income, you might take a course or two to improve. While you can't do anything about your birth year, you might better position yourself to capitalize on x factors. For example, you can focus on developing new relationships or try to take advantage of a major economic or industry shift. All these examples point to the same necessary occurrence; to improve your finances and position in life, you will need to make at least one major change. Secondly, I encourage you to keep learning and experimenting with wealth concepts. I recommend reading *Think and Grow Rich* and *The Millionaire Next Door.*

Napoleon Hill conducted the first widely published study of affluent individuals in his bestselling classic *Think and Grow Rich*, released in 1937. Hill studied more than five hundred self-made American millionaires over a span of twenty years. His interviews and research culminated in thirteen principles to achieve riches and fulfillment. The thirteen principles mainly address an individual's mind-set, habits, and personality traits. For instance, they address how desire, faith, and specialized knowledge influence finances.

Another well-known book to tackle the topic of prosperity is the bestseller *The Millionaire Next Door*. Thomas Stanley and William Danko surveyed and studied thousands of high-net-worth individuals (HNWI) over twenty years. Their masterpiece reveals profiles, attitudes, and behaviors relating to a variety of wealth-related subjects, including financial, career, and family planning. They highlight seven factors that are instrumental to building wealth. For example, well-off individuals value financial independence above displaying high social status.

Researching affluent individuals has dramatically altered my perspectives on career and lifestyle. Money is important—we need it to survive but we should ask ourselves how much is enough? I want to have enough money to be financially free, but not too much that it causes problems or headaches. Therefore, my goal isn't to become a billionaire because it's unrealistic given how I want to live my life (and the probability is low). For example, I don't want work all hours of the day like Jeff Bezos or go years without a vacation like Mark Cuban. Furthermore, amassing riches usually requires many personal sacrifices, which can lead to regrets and poor health.

You should consider what your objectives are and how much money you need to support them. Also, other factors, skills, and habits are necessary to build wealth. People who make good incomes, invest wisely, and live well below their means are million-dollar candidates, for example.

Only a small percentage of people get extremely promising starts in life, but that doesn't mean the rest of us can't finish how we want. Building wealth isn't easy, but it can and has been done—even when we begin at the starting line with everyone else. You are the money you want to make, the lifestyle you want to live, and the success you want to achieve.

To your financial prosperity,

— Chad E. Tennant

To learn about my new books, please join my new book club (www.chadtennant.com/new-book-club), and follow my Amazon author page (www.amazon.com/Chad-E.-Tennant/e/B0758WKWSC).

Please take a few seconds to leave a review on Amazon. Your feedback is appreciated!

Made in the USA
Lexington, KY
13 December 2017

DEC 20 2017 #7.99